BE A
SALES
SUPERSTAR

BE A
SALES
SUPERSTAR

21 GREAT WAYS TO SELL MORE, FASTER, EASIER IN TOUGH MARKETS

BRIAN TRACY

BK

BERRETT–KOEHLER PUBLISHERS, INC.
San Francisco

Berrett-Koehler Publishers, Inc.
235 Montgomery Street, Suite 650
San Francisco, CA 94104-2916
Tel: (415) 288-0260   Fax: (415) 362-2512   www.bkconnection.com

ORDERING INFORMATION

Quantity sales. Special discounts are available on quantity purchases by corporations, associations, and others. For details, contact the "Special Sales Department" at the Berrett-Koehler address above.

Individual sales. Berrett-Koehler publications are available through most bookstores. They can also be ordered direct from Berrett-Koehler: Tel: (800) 929-2929; Fax: (802) 864-7626; www.bkconnection.com

Orders for college textbook/course adoption use. Please contact Berrett-Koehler: Tel: (800) 929-2929; Fax: (802) 864-7626.

Orders by U.S. trade bookstores and wholesalers. Please contact Publishers Group West, 1700 Fourth Street, Berkeley, CA 94710. Tel: (510) 528-1444; Fax: (510) 528-3444.

Printed in the United States of America

 Printed on acid-free and recycled paper that is composed of 50% recovered fiber, including 10% postconsumer waste.

Library of Congress Cataloging-in-Publication Data
Tracy, Brian.
    Be a sales superstar : 21 greatest ways to sell more, faster, easier, in tough markets / by Brian Tracy.
        p. cm.
    Includes bibliographical references and index.
    ISBN 1-57675-175-9
    1. Selling. 2. Sales personnel. I. Title.
HF5438.25 .T712 2002
658.85—dc21   2002018375

Copyediting and proofreading by PeopleSpeak.
Book design and composition by Beverly Butterfield, Girl of the West Productions.

FIRST EDITION
07 06 05 04 03   10 9 8 7 6 5

This book is dedicated to my dear friend and
business partner Ib Moller, a great entrepreneur,
a superb sales professional, an excellent executive,
and a fine person in every way.

Contents

Preface

This book is for ambitious salespeople who are eager to increase their sales and boost their incomes immediately. It is written for those who are, or intend to be, in the top 10 percent of their fields in selling. Every idea is aimed at the sales superstars of today and tomorrow.

Salespeople are primarily motivated by two things: money and status. They want to be paid well, and they measure their success by the size of their incomes relative to others'. In addition, they want to be recognized and appreciated for their efforts and for their successes. This book will show salespeople how to make quantum leaps in both areas.

Most salespeople have never been professionally trained in selling. Fully 95 percent of salespeople can increase their sales with additional knowledge and skill. Sometimes you are only one skill away from becoming a sales superstar. This book will help you to identify that skill and begin the process of mastering it.

Occasionally, I begin a seminar or talk by asking, "How many people here today are in sales?" Invariably, only a few hands go up. I pause and wait for a few seconds and then I ask, "Who here is *really* in sales?"

Suddenly, they get it. More and more hands go up until almost every hand in the room is raised. I then go on to say, "That's right. Everyone is in sales, no matter what you do. Your entire life is a continuous process of communicating, persuading, and influencing other people. The only question is, How good are you in these areas?"

Your ability to "sell" others on your ideas will determine your success in your life and career as much as any other factor. If your income and success actually depend on selling, what you will learn in the pages to follow can change your life.

I wrote this book to give you, a busy sales professional, a handbook that you could refer to quickly to pick up key ideas and techniques that would immediately increase your effectiveness and boost your results. As it happens, more than 4,000 books on selling are available today and almost all of them are valuable and worthwhile.

What makes this book different?

The answer is that this book is short and straight to the point. In 144 pages, you will learn twenty-one of the most important principles for sales success that

I have discovered in the training of more than 500,000 sales professionals in twenty-three countries. Each of these strategies is tested and proven to work. Any one of these ideas can boost your sales and income immediately.

When I began selling, knocking on doors, going from office to office, cold-calling, I learned a concept called the "Winning Edge Principle." This is one of the great insights to success in every area of life, including selling.

The principle says this: *Small differences in ability in key areas can lead to enormous differences in results.*

Small improvements in important sales skills, such as prospecting, making persuasive presentations, overcoming objections, or closing the sale, can lead to huge increases in sales results. This book is designed to show you specific techniques that will enable you to make those jumps in performance, to give you the "winning edge."

Here is another key idea for success: *Your weakest important skill sets the height at which you can use all your other skills and determines your income.*

In other words, if you are poor in a key skill area such as prospecting or closing, that one weakness alone will determine your sales results and how much you earn. A single deficiency in your ability can hold you back from succeeding, no matter how good you might be in every other area.

Put another way, your *strengths* have brought you to where you are today, but your *weaknesses* are now holding you back from progressing further and faster.

This book is designed to give you sales tools you can use to overcome any critical weakness you may have—first, by identifying it and second, by giving you practical exercises you can apply immediately to strengthen yourself in that area.

This book deals simultaneously with both the *inner* game of selling, the mental component, and the *outer* game of selling, the methods and techniques of actually making the sale. When you begin to improve in both areas together, both your sales and your self-confidence will increase at a rapid rate.

Only small differences in attitude and ability separate the top salespeople from the average. When you learn and apply the twenty-one great ways to be a sales superstar, you will quickly move to the top of your field. Your future in selling will become unlimited.

BRIAN TRACY
Solana Beach, California
February 2002

Introduction: Think Like a Top Salesperson

This is a wonderful time to be alive and working in the profession of selling. Regardless of the ups and downs of the economy or temporary changes in your industry, there have never been more opportunities for you to achieve more of your goals—and enjoy a higher standard of living—than exist today by selling more of your products and services in the marketplace. And if anything, as you continually upgrade your skills, your situation is going to get better and better in the months and years ahead.

The better you become at selling, the more opportunities will open up for you. According to Dr. Thomas Stanley, coauthor of *The Millionaire Next Door,* fully 5 percent of self-made millionaires in America are salespeople who have sold for another company all their lives. The way they became millionaires was quite straightforward. First, they became very good at selling. Second, they earned an excellent living as a result. And third, they saved and invested a substantial part of their incomes as they went along. So can you.

My personal story in the field of selling is similar to that of many others. I started off with limited opportunities. My parents never had very much money. My father worked as a carpenter and my mother was a nurse, but they were not always regularly employed. I didn't graduate from high school. In fact, I behaved so badly in high school that I was suspended and eventually expelled from three different schools.

When I left high school, the only work I could get was laboring jobs. I washed dishes in the back of a small hotel, stacked lumber in a sawmill, dug wells, and worked as a construction laborer, carrying heavy materials from one place to another. I worked on farms and ranches and as a galley boy on a ship in the North Atlantic. Finally, when I couldn't get a laboring job, I drifted into straight commission sales, selling office supplies from door to door.

I wasn't afraid to work, but hard work alone didn't seem to be enough. I made hundreds of calls without making any sales. I used to run from office to office and from door to door so that I could see more people. But I was just barely hanging on by my fingernails.

Then one day I began to ask, "Why is it that some salespeople are more successful than others?" I heard that the top 20 percent of salespeople in every field earned 80 percent of the money. The top 10 percent earned even more. So I did something that changed my life.

I went to the top salesman in my company and asked him what he was doing differently from me. And he told me. He told me how to ask questions and how to develop a sales presentation. He told me how to respond to objections and to ask for orders. I then went out and did what he told me to do and my sales went up.

Then I learned that there were books on selling. I bought them one after another and began to study the subject of selling one to two hours every morning before I started out. And my sales went up even more. Then I learned about audio programs and sales seminars. As I listened to audio programs continually and attended every seminar I could find, I learned what the best salespeople had taken years to learn. And my sales continued to increase.

In less than one year, I went from calling door to door, making one or two small sales per week, to managing a six-country sales organization and earning thousands of dollars a month. The key was simple. I just found out how other top salespeople sold. I then did the same things that the top people were doing until I got the same results that they were getting. This method has worked for everyone who has ever tried it, and it will work for you as well.

The great law of human destiny, especially in sales, is the *Law of Cause and Effect*. This law says that for everything that happens, there is a reason or reasons. If you want a particular goal, or *effect,* in your life, you can have it. Simply seek out someone else who has already achieved that particular effect or result, and then find out what he or she did to get it. If you then do the same things that the other person did, you will eventually get the same results. This cause-and-effect principle explains exactly how people have gone from failure to success in every field of endeavor throughout history.

The most important application of the Law of Cause and Effect is this: *Thoughts are causes and conditions are effects.*

Your outer world tends to be a reflection of your inner world. You invariably attract into your life the people, the circumstances, the opportunities, and even the sales that are in harmony with your dominant thoughts. As you change your thinking about yourself and your possibilities, you change your life. This is the way the law works.

Perhaps the most important discovery in human history, the foundation of all religions, philosophies, metaphysics, and psychology, is this: *You become what you think about most of the time.*

Just think! You become what you think about most of the time. Your outer world eventually corresponds to your inner world. And since only you can decide what it is you think about, you are the person who ultimately determines what happens to you in life.

Over a period of twenty-five years, in research conducted by Dr. Martin Seligman at the University of

Pennsylvania, more than 350,000 salespeople were interviewed to find out what they think about most of the time. Their incomes were compared with their thought patterns to determine what kind of thinking patterns most accurately predict the highest incomes.

And do you know what the top salespeople think about most of the time? It's simple. They think about what they *want* and *how* to get it. They think and talk, all day long, about their goals and how to achieve their goals. And because the more you think and talk about your goals, the more positive and enthusiastic you become, these salespeople seem to sell five and ten times as much as the *average* person, who thinks about his or her problems most of the time.

The rule is this: If you think like the top salespeople think, you will eventually do the things that the top salespeople do, and you will get the same results that the top salespeople get. And if you don't, you won't. It is as simple as that.

Some salespeople are satisfied earning $25,000 a year. This is consistent with the way they think most of the time. This is their financial "comfort zone." Other salespeople would be dissatisfied if their incomes dropped below $100,000 a year. This is their comfort zone.

Researchers have discovered that there is very little difference between the people who are earning a small amount and the people who are earning a huge amount. They have very much the same levels of talent and ability. They are surrounded with very much the same number of opportunities and possibilities. The only difference is that the highest paid salespeople have *decided* to earn that amount, and the only question they ask—all day long—is, How?

According to the studies, the most important single quality for great success in selling is the quality of *optimism.* Top salespeople are far more optimistic than average people. Because of this optimism, they have high expectations of success. Because they confidently expect to be successful, they make more calls on more prospects than the average salesperson. In addition, because they expect to succeed eventually, they persist much longer. They call back more often. They believe that their success is inevitable. It is only a matter of time, as long as they keep calling and calling back.

As a result of calling on more people in the first place and calling back more often, they make more sales. When they make more sales, their success reinforces their belief in the value of making more calls and calling back more often. This process, repeated over and over, becomes a habit of high performance. This habit assures that they move higher and higher in income and personal success.

Here is another key point in superstar selling: Your self-esteem is directly related to how much you sell.

The highest paid and most successful salespeople have high levels of self-esteem. Self-esteem is best defined as *how much you like yourself.* The more you like yourself, the better you do. The better you do, the more you like yourself. Each reinforces the other.

The more you like yourself, the higher goals and standards you set for yourself. The more you like yourself, the greater is your confidence in your ability to succeed and the more likely you are to persist in the face of adversity. The more you like yourself, the more others will like you and the more open they will be to buying from you and recommending you to their friends.

Here is an important parallel. Mental fitness is very much like physical fitness. If you do certain physical exercises each day, you will eventually become very fit *physically*. By the same token, if you do certain mental exercises every day, you will soon become very fit *mentally*. You will develop high levels of self-esteem and self-confidence and a positive mental attitude.

Therefore, the starting point of great success in selling is for you to begin to *think* the way top salespeople think. Each time you think the way a top salesperson thinks, you become more optimistic and creative. You feel happier and more effective. You experience more energy and determination. You make more calls and better presentations. You close more sales and you make more money. When you learn and practice the mental qualities of top salespeople, your whole life opens up for you like a summer sunrise. Let's begin.

Commit to Excellence

Make it a life-rule to give your best
to whatever passes through your hands.
Stamp it with your personal character.
Let superiority be your trademark.

—ORISON SWETT MARDEN

Optimists, people with high expectations of eventual success, are *ambitious*. The more optimistic they are, the more ambitious and determined they become. Ambition is therefore the most important single expression of optimism, and it is the key quality for the achievement of great success in sales or in any other field. Ambition is so important to goal setting, courage, and persistence that having this one quality alone can almost guarantee that you will overcome every obstacle and difficulty that stands in your way.

Ambitious people have one remarkable character-
istic in sales. They dream big dreams. They have high
aspirations. They see themselves as capable of *being
the best* in their fields. They know that the top 20 percent of salespeople make 80 percent of the sales, and
they are determined to be among that top group.

Ambitious salespeople are optimistic about their
opportunities and possibilities. They are absolutely
convinced that they can achieve their goals by selling
substantial amounts of their products or services. And
they are completely determined to do it. The only
question they ask is, How?

Perhaps the most important step you can take in
the field of selling is to commit yourself to personal
excellence, to becoming one of the best in your field.
Resolve today that you are going to join the top 20 percent in your industry, and then the top 10 percent, in
terms of sales and earnings.

Here is an insight that changed my life when I
was twenty-eight years old. After years of hard work
and struggle, it suddenly dawned on me: *Everyone
who is in the top 10 percent today started in the bottom
10 percent!*

Everyone who is doing well today was once doing
poorly. Everyone who is at the top of your field was
once not even in your field at all. Everybody who is
at the front of the buffet line of life started at the back
of the line.

Now, here is the question: How do you get to the front of the buffet line of life, where all the good stuff is waiting for you? The answer is simple. It consists of two key steps: First, get in line! Second, stay in line!

It is absolutely amazing the number of people who want to get to the front of the buffet line of life—who admire or envy the people who are already up there enjoying the best that life has to offer—but don't get up and get in line themselves. They don't realize that life, like a buffet, is *self-serve.*

The way that you *get in line* is by making a decision that you are going to be excellent in your field and then by taking action to learn and apply whatever knowledge and skills you need to get ahead.

Once you get in line, the way that you then get to the front of the buffet line of life is to *stay in line!* Once you have made the decision to be among the very best in your field, get in line and stay in line. Keep putting one foot in front of the other. Keep developing new skills and acquiring new knowledge each day, each week, each month. Keep improving at your craft of selling. Keep moving forward.

The good news is the buffet line of life and success never closes! It stays open and continues to move twenty-four hours a day. If you get in line and stay in line, if you start moving and refuse to quit, nothing and no one can stop you. You must eventually get to the front of the line in your profession. You must eventually become one of the most skilled and highest paid people in your field if you make a total commitment to excellence and then never go back on your commitment.

Here is the turning point in your life: *Make a decision!* The dividing line between success and failure is contained in your ability to make a clear, unequivocal decision that you are going to *be the best* and then to back your decision with persistence and determination until you reach your goal.

The world is full of people who are wishing, hoping, and praying for their lives to be better, but they never make the kind of *do or die* decision that leads to great success.

Just as you become what you *think* about most of the time, you also become what you say to yourself on a regular basis. You should repeat to yourself, over and over again, the words *"I'm the best! I'm the best! I'm the best!"* until they come true in your life. And they surely will.

ACTION EXERCISES

Make a list of all the things you do each day that contribute to your sales. Describe in detail the sales process from the initial prospecting to the completed sale and the satisfied customer.

Review this list and give yourself a grade from one to ten in each skill area. Have your boss evaluate you as well.

Then ask yourself this question: "What one skill, if I developed and did it consistently in an excellent fashion, would have the greatest positive impact on my sales?"

This is the key question for moving ahead in the line. Ask your boss. Ask your coworkers. Ask your customers. But find out the answer. Then, set the development of this skill as a goal: write it down, set a deadline, make a plan, and work on becoming better at this key skill every day until you master it.

Act As If It Were Impossible to Fail

Courage is resistance to fear,

mastery of fear—not absence of fear.

—MARK TWAIN

Fear, uncertainty, and doubt are, and always have been, the greatest enemies of success and happiness. For this reason, top salespeople work continually to confront the fears that hold most salespeople back. The two major fears that stand as the greatest obstacles on your road to success are the fear of *failure*, or loss, and the fear of *criticism*, or rejection. These are the major enemies to be overcome.

As it happens, it is not the actual failure or rejection that hurts you or holds you back. It is the *fear* of failure or rejection that stops you from acting. It is the anticipation or expectation of failure or rejection that paralyzes you and blocks you from doing what you need to do to achieve your goals.

The truth is that everyone is afraid of something, and often, many things. Everyone you meet is afraid of failure and rejection in some way. The difference between a hero and a coward is that the hero is brave just a couple of minutes longer. The average person moves away from and avoids the fear-causing situation. A brave person forces himself or herself to confront the fear and do what is feared anyway.

Glenn Ford, the actor, once said, *"If you do not do the thing you fear, then the fear controls your life."*

Ralph Waldo Emerson said his entire life was changed when he read the words *"If you would be a great success, make a habit throughout your life of doing the things you fear."*

The fear of failure, the major obstacle that holds you back, is felt in the solar plexus and experienced as the feeling of "I can't!"

You can neutralize this feeling by repeating the opposite phrase, "I can! I can!" over and over. Even more effective for neutralizing the fear of failure is to say to yourself "I can do it! I can do it!" over and over, until you actually believe it.

Whenever you repeat the words "I can do it!" your fears go down and your self-confidence goes up. When you repeat to yourself the words "I like myself! I'm the best! I can do it!" you boost your self-esteem and self-image to the point where eventually you feel *unstoppable.* You create within yourself the mind-set of a high performance salesperson.

Then, as Emerson said, "Do the thing and you will have the power."

Here is a key point about fear of any kind. Instead of waiting until you feel courageous enough, do the thing you fear, and the courage will come afterward. As Aristotle said, "Act as if you already had the quality you desire, and you shall have it."

◆

ACTION EXERCISES

Identify the one great fear that holds you back from throwing your whole heart into becoming a big success in your field. There is always at least one fear lurking in the back of your mind.

Now imagine that you do not have this fear at all. Imagine that you are totally unafraid in every part of your sales work. Imagine that you are guaranteed complete success in everything you do. How would you act or behave if you had no fears at all?

Whatever your answer, from now on act as it if were impossible to fail, and it shall be! Fake it until you make it.

Put Your Whole Heart into Your Selling

*You are never given a wish
without also being given the
power to make it come true.*

—RICHARD BACH

Top salespeople believe in their companies. They believe in their products and services, and they believe in their customers. Above all, they believe in themselves and their ability to succeed.

Your level of belief in the value of a product or service is directly related to your ability to convince other people that it is good for them. Selling has often been called a *transfer of enthusiasm*. The more enthusiastic and convinced you are about what you are selling, the more contagious this enthusiasm will be and the more your customers will sense it and act on it.

19

Human beings are primarily emotional in everything they do and say. This is why *caring* is a critical element in successful selling. You've heard it said that people *don't care how much you know until they know how much you care.* What we also know is that the more you love your work, the more caring you will be. The more committed you are to your company and to your products and services, the more you will naturally and honestly care about your customers. The more you honestly care about your company and your customers, the more concerned you will be about helping customers to make a good buying decision.

Since you become what you think about most of the time, you should repeat the words "I love my work! I love my work! I love my work!" over and over. The more you say these words to yourself, the more you will like yourself as a salesperson and enjoy your selling activities. The more you enjoy your work, the better you will do it and the more committed you will be to your customers. Selling will become easier and easier and more rewarding in every way.

My favorite affirmation, which I still use continually, is *"I like myself and I love my work!"* I use these words to get me up and going in the morning and keep me going throughout the day. The more I repeat them, the better and more confident I feel about myself and everything I am doing. Try them yourself and see.

All top salespeople like themselves and love their work. And their customers can feel it. As a result, their customers want to buy from them, buy from them again, and recommend them to their friends.

ACTION EXERCISES

If you want to feel enthusiastic, act enthusiastic! Imagine that your products and services were the very best quality and the very best priced in the entire world. How would you behave in every customer interaction, all day long?

Put your whole heart into your sales work. Imagine that you were being videotaped and that this video was going to be shown nationwide as a shining example of an outstanding salesperson in action. How would you treat every customer or prospect? Whatever your answer, practice that behavior every hour of every day.

Position Yourself as a Real Professional

The self image is the key to

human personality and human behavior.

Change the self image and you change

the personality and the behavior.

—MAXWELL MALTZ

Top salespeople see themselves as *consultants* rather than as salespeople. They see themselves as advisors, helpers, counselors, and friends to their clients and customers. They see themselves as problem solvers more than anything else.

Perhaps the most important single determinant of whether or not someone buys from you is how that person thinks and feels about you. In marketing, this is called "positioning." The position you have in the heart and mind of your customer is determined by the words that your customer uses when he or she thinks about you and describes you to others when you are not there.

Many tens of thousands of customers have been asked how they think and feel about the top salespeople who sell to them. The most common answer that customers give is that they see the best salespeople more as *consultants* than as salespeople. They see them as valuable knowledge resources in their personal and business lives.

They trust these top professionals to give them good advice in their areas of product or service specialization. Once a customer views you as a *consultant* and as a friend, he or she will never buy from anyone else, no matter what the small differences might be in price or product/service features.

Early in my career I discovered an amazing psychological principle. I found that people largely accept you, at least initially, at your own evaluation of yourself. In other words, whatever you say about yourself, however you describe yourself, people will usually accept without argument. They will then watch your behavior to make sure that what you say about yourself and the way you behave are consistent with each other.

For example, if you tell me that you are always punctual, I will believe you. I have no reason not to. I will then observe your actual behavior to see how punctual you are. If your behavior is consistent with your claim, I then will accept this as a true statement about you.

When I first learned this principle with regard to being a *consultant,* I decided to practice it immediately. Up to that time, I had been introducing myself as a salesman, with mixed results and reactions from my prospects. At my very next appointment, I said to my prospect, "Thank you for your time. Please relax. I'm not really here to sell you anything. *I see myself more as a consultant than as a salesperson,* and all I really want to do is ask you a couple of questions and see if my company can help you in a cost-effective way. But *I see myself more as a consultant than as a salesperson."*

From the very first time I described myself as a consultant, my customers treated me differently. They invited me in for coffee and invited me out for lunch. They listened to me far more attentively and were far more open with me when I asked them questions about their needs. They bought from me far more readily and recommended me to their friends. They invited me home to have dinner with their families and placed me in an entirely new category in their minds. And I was only twenty-four years old!

From now on, think of yourself as a consultant. Walk, talk, and behave like a consultant. Dress, groom, and prepare for every sales meeting as if you were a highly paid and competent consultant and advisor in your field—because you are. When people ask you what you do, tell them proudly "I'm a consultant."

I taught this principle not long ago to the manager of a company that sold roofing and shingles. He liked the idea so much, he went back to the office, gathered up all the salespeople's business cards and replaced them with new cards that had the words "Exterior Cladding Consultant" on them. He told me that within thirty days, the atmosphere in his whole company changed. The salespeople began treating each other differently. They behaved differently toward their customers as well when they saw themselves as consultants. In the first month after this change, their sales increased 32 percent.

Remember the first rule of self-image psychology: The person you *see* is the person you will *be*. Your self-image, the person you see yourself as on the *inside*, will determine how you behave on the *outside*.

The best positioning you can have among your prospects and customers is that of an expert, an authority in your area of expertise. Your customers look to you, as a consultant, to give them valuable advice they can use to improve their work or life in a cost-effective way. When you walk, talk, and act like a consultant, you set yourself apart from people who see themselves as salespeople. You begin moving into the top 10 percent in your field.

ACTION EXERCISES

From this moment forward, see yourself as a consultant in your profession and for your company. Instead of trying to *sell* your products or services, *ask* good questions about what your prospects are doing today and look for ways to help them achieve their goals with what you sell.

Position yourself as a consultant, working for and with a prospect to advise him or her on the right course of action. Use words like "we" and "us" and "our." Make suggestions and recommendations such as "What I would recommend that we do now is the following." Be a helper and a counselor rather than a salesperson.

Above all, position yourself as a problem solver. Focus on identifying a problem of the prospect for which your product or service is the ideal solution. Then show the prospect how much better off he or she can be by using what you sell.

Prepare Thoroughly for Every Call

If you employed study, thinking and
planning time daily, you could develop
and use the power that could change
the course of your destiny.

—W. CLEMENT STONE

Preparation is the mark of the professional—in every field. The highest paid salespeople review every detail of an account before every sales call. They study their notes from previous calls. They read the literature and information they have gathered on the prospect. And their prospects can sense it almost immediately.

On the other hand, the lowest paid salespeople try to get by with the very minimum of preparation. They go into a sales meeting and attempt to "wing it."

They think that the prospect will not notice. But prospects and customers are very aware if a person has come in unprepared. Don't let this happen to you.

Your goal is to be among the top 10 percent of salespeople in your field. To reach that goal, you must do what the top people do, over and over, until it is as natural to you as breathing. And the top people prepare thoroughly, every single time.

Preparation for great success in selling consists of three parts. They are precall research, precall objectives, and postcall analysis. Let us discuss them in order.

Precall Analysis

During this stage, you gather all the information about the prospect and/or the prospect's company that you possibly can. Check the Internet, the local library, newspapers, and other sources. If you're gathering information on a company, either visit it or ask someone at the company to send you the most recent brochures and sales materials that the company uses for its own marketing. Read all this material and make notes of key points. The more precall research you do, the more intelligent and informed you will sound when you finally sit down with the prospect.

If you are dealing with a business, make it a point to find out everything you can about its products, services, history, competitors, and current activities. The rule is that you should never ask a question of a prospect if the information is readily available elsewhere. Nothing undermines your credibility more rapidly than for you to ask something like "What do you do here?"

This type of question tells the prospect that you have not bothered to do any research before the call. This is definitely not the kind of message you want to send at your first meeting.

Precall Objectives

The second part of preparation is where you set your *precall objectives*. This is the stage where you think through and plan your coming sales call in detail, in advance. Imagine that your sales manager were riding along with you and prior to the sales call, he asked you, "Who are you going to see, what are you going to ask, and what results do you hope to achieve from this sales call?"

Whatever your answers would be to that question, think them through before you see the prospect. Write them down. The best exercise of all is for you to prepare a list of questions, in order, that you are going to ask the prospect when you meet with him or her. Customers love salespeople who are thoroughly prepared with a written outline when they make a sales call.

Here is a great technique used by many of the top sales professionals. Prepare an "agenda" for the sales call before you go. Make a list of questions you would like to ask, in sequence, from the general to the particular. Space them out on the page so there is room for the prospect to make notes.

When you meet with your prospect, say, "Thank you for your time. I know how busy you are. I have prepared an agenda for our meeting with some questions that we can go over. Here is your copy."

Customers love this approach. It shows that you are respectful of their time and that you have prepared for the meeting in advance. You then follow the agenda, asking the listed questions and asking additional questions that come up. Properly carried out, this method can be amazingly helpful in positioning yourself in your prospect's mind as a true professional and as a consultant rather than as a salesperson.

Postcall Analysis

The third part of preparation is your *postcall analysis.* Immediately after the call, take a few moments to write down every bit of information that you can recall from the recent discussion. Don't trust this to your memory, and don't wait until the end of the day. Write down every single fact you can remember as quickly as you can. You will be surprised at how helpful these notes will become in the development of the prospect into a customer.

Then, prior to seeing the customer again, take a few minutes and review all of your notes. I think of this as "fluffing up your mental pillow." When you do, you will be alert and fully prepared regarding this customer and his or her situation.

Customers are always impressed when they are called upon by a truly professional salesperson who remembers clearly what was discussed at their last meeting and who has obviously done his or her homework.

Your willingness and ability to prepare thoroughly are critical to your long-term success and to earning the kind of money you want to earn. The rule is this: When in doubt, *overprepare!* You will never regret being too prepared for a sales call. Often, your efforts in preparation will be the key factor that gets you the sale.

◆

ACTION EXERCISES

Prepare a checklist of questions that you will need to ask to determine whether a prospect is a likely customer for what you sell. Review this checklist prior to every first meeting and use it as a guide to keep yourself organized and on track.

Prepare an "agenda" for an upcoming sales meeting. Put it on your company letterhead. Put the prospect's name, company, and time and date of the appointment at the top. Present an unfolded, clean copy to the prospect at the beginning of the meeting, and then follow the agenda during the conversation. You will be delighted at the results.

Dedicate Yourself to Continuous Learning

You can learn anything you need to learn to achieve any goal you can set for yourself; there are no limits.

—BRIAN TRACY

To earn more, you must learn more. You are "maxed out" today at your current level of knowledge and skill. You cannot get more or better results by simply working harder using your present abilities. If you want to earn more in the future, you must learn and apply new methods and techniques. Remember the old saying: "The more you do of what you're doing, the more you'll get of what you're getting."

The fact is that we are experiencing an explosion of knowledge and technology that is unprecedented in human history. These advances are creating new competitors and driving our existing competition to develop better, faster, cheaper ways to get business. This is why continuous learning is the minimum requirement for success in selling today.

The future belongs to the learners, not just to the hard workers. The highest paid salespeople spend much more time and money improving themselves and upgrading their skills than the average salesperson. As a result, they earn vastly more in any market, sometimes five and ten times as much.

At a seminar in San Diego recently, a salesman came up to me and told me an interesting story. He said that he was one of the top salespeople in his field, if not in his industry. He had regularly earned more than $100,000 per year and was highly respected by both his boss and his peers.

A year before, his boss had urged him to listen to my audio program "The Psychology of Selling." He initially refused, saying that he didn't need it. He was already doing better than most other people in his field.

Finally, he gave in and ordered the program, with the intention of listening to it once and then sending it back. When he received the program, he not only listened to it once, he listened again and again, month after month. In that one year, by practicing the ideas contained in that $70 program, he increased his personal income by $70,000, a return on his investment of 1,000 times!

Continuous learning is like an ongoing mental fitness program for sales champions, where you prepare and keep yourself in shape for intense competition. This is the attitude possessed by the highest paid people in the business.

Fortunately, keeping yourself at the top of your game in selling is much easier than in professional athletics. Sales fitness requires daily brainwork and application rather than the hours of sweating and hard physical exercise required for athletic competition. No matter how hard you work on developing yourself, you don't have to take a shower afterward.

A continuous learning program in selling has three key parts. Consistent, persistent work in these three areas will lead inevitably to your becoming one of the highest paid salespeople in your field, with no exceptions. I have given this advice to hundreds of thousands of salespeople and not one of them has ever come back and said that this strategy didn't work. In many cases, salespeople have doubled and tripled their incomes in as little as thirty days by the daily practice of these three continuous learning principles.

Leaders Are Readers

The first principle is simply for you to read continually in your field. Get up earlier each morning and read for one hour about selling. Put the newspaper aside. Leave the television off. Instead, read, underline, and make notes in a good book on selling strategies and tactics. Look for practical ideas you can use immediately. Turn them over in your mind. Imagine using them in your sales activities. Then, throughout the day, practice what you learned in the morning.

Sometimes people ask me what books to read. The answer is simple. Begin by asking other top salespeople for their recommendations. Almost all top salespeople have their own collections of sales books. There are currently more than 4,000 books on selling in print, with 50 to 100 new books coming onto the market each year. Begin building your own collection today.

If you read about selling for one hour each day, that will amount to about one book per week. One book per week will add up to 50 books per year. Since the average salesperson reads less than one sales book per year, if you were to read 50 books per year, that alone would give you "the winning edge" that will move you to the top of your sales force.

To earn a doctorate from a university, you would be required to read and distill 30 to 50 books into a dissertation that would synthesize the key ideas of these books into a new form. If you were to read and synthesize the best ideas of 30 to 50 books on selling every twelve months, you would achieve the equivalent of a doctorate in professional selling each year. You would probably become one of the best-informed and most competent salespeople of your generation in no time at all, just by reading one hour per day.

If you read 50 sales books per year for the next ten years, that would amount to 500 books. At the very least, you would need a new house just to hold your books, and you would be able to afford it as well.

Listen and Learn

The second part of continuous learning is for you to listen to audio programs in your car. Audio learning has been described as "the greatest advance in education since the invention of the printing press."

As a sales professional, you spend between 500 and 1,000 hours behind the wheel each year. This amounts to between twelve and twenty-five 40-hour weeks per annum, or the equivalent of three to six months of working time in your car each year. Twelve to twenty-five 40-hour weeks is equal to one to two full-time university semesters that you spend driving each year.

According to the University of Southern California, you can get the equivalent of full-time university attendance by listening to educational audio programs as you drive from place to place.

Turn your car into a learning machine, into a "university on wheels." Enroll at "automobile university" and attend full time for the rest of your career. It can change your life, as it has changed mine.

A young salesman in Pittsburgh approached me at a seminar recently and told me his story. He said that he got his first sales job when he finished college four years before. To start him off, his boss gave him "Psychology of Selling" to listen to in his car.

But he didn't like to listen to audio programs in his car. He preferred to listen to music as he went from call to call, a behavior practiced by most lower level salespeople, who earn little and who are going nowhere in their careers.

He therefore took the audio program and put it in the trunk of his car. Whenever his boss asked him if he was listening to the program, he replied, "I carry it in my car all the time!"

At the end of his first year, his boss called him in and told him he was going to have to let him go. He was the lowest selling salesperson in the company during a period when the industry was booming and everyone else was doing well. The boss gave him thirty days' notice to clear up his accounts and hand over his prospects to other salespeople.

At the end of the meeting, the boss asked curiously, "Did you ever listen to Brian Tracy's audio program? I can't imagine that you could be doing so poorly if you had practiced some of those ideas."

The young salesman, Bill, told me that he felt terrible. He couldn't look his boss in the eye. There he was being fired from his first job for poor performance, and he had been misleading his boss about listening to a simple audio program for an entire year. His income for the last twelve months was only $22,000. And he was a college graduate!

He went out to his car and got the program from the trunk. He resolved to listen to the first cassette on the way home so that he could at least look his boss in the eye. He stuck the tape into the player as he left the parking lot and began to listen.

He told me that that experience was a transforming moment in his life. He had never listened to an educational audio program before. He was amazed at how many good ideas were contained on a single tape. He kept starting and stopping it, rewinding and replaying key parts, all the way home.

He began to understand why he had done so poorly in sales in the previous year. He had good product knowledge but no idea whatsoever about how to prospect, qualify, identify needs, make a professional presentation, or ask for the order. He had thought that selling was something that came naturally. He realized, for the first time, that selling was both an art and a science, with a specific methodology and process.

He listened to my program nonstop, every driving moment. By the end of that month, his sales had jumped. His boss gave him one more month. In the next thirty days, his sales increased again and he was taken off probation. The next month, his sales went up again. He was on his way.

He listened to the audio program over and over, before and after every sales call. He learned how to get more and better telephone appointments, how to make better presentations, answer objections, and get more referrals from his customers. He learned how to deal with price concerns and how to close the sale thirty-two different ways. And with each new technique he learned and practiced, his sales and his confidence increased.

In his second year, he made $46,000. In his third year, he earned $94,000. In his fourth year in selling, he had earned $175,000. He was already on track to make $250,000 in the coming year.

"Last night," he said, "I picked up my first new car, a Mercedes, and drove it to this seminar to celebrate. Continuous learning changed my life, and I still listen to audio programs every minute that I am in my car."

When we were teenagers, we got into the habit of driving around with our friends and listening to music. We formed the association that driving is for friends and fun. Many adults never get over this conditioned behavior. Instead, at a time of incredible competition, information explosion, and obsolescence of knowledge, they are still floating through life, driving around, failing to take advantage of one of the very best learning methodologies ever discovered.

Don't let this happen to you. Never let your car be running without educational audio programs playing. Make every minute count. One great idea or technique can change the course of your career and dramatically increase your income.

Learn from the Experts

The third part of continuous learning is for you to take all the training you can get. Attend seminars and courses on professional selling. Ask for advice from others on the most helpful courses they have taken. Be aggressive about seeking out training in your community, and be prepared to travel if necessary. Many of the top salespeople I know will fly hundreds and even thousands of miles to attend sales conferences. And the difference that it makes in their sales results is amazing.

My life, and the lives of many of the highest paid professionals I know, has been changed dramatically as the result of attending a single sales course, boot camp, or seminar. Sometimes the ideas and strategies contained in one program have catapulted a person from rags to riches.

Practice the 3 Percent Rule

Here is a rule that will guarantee your success—and possibly make you rich: *Invest 3 percent of your income back into yourself.* Invest 3 percent of however much you earn back into becoming even better at what you did to earn the money in the first place.

When you begin investing in yourself regularly, your whole attitude toward yourself, your future, and your finances will change for the better. You will become more skilled and knowledgeable. You will become more serious about your craft and your customers. You will respect yourself more and be more respected by others.

For every dollar you invest back into yourself to improve your ability to earn even more, you will get a return of ten, twenty, fifty, one hundred, and even one thousand times your investment. Sometimes, in one paragraph of a book, one side of an audio program, or one session of a seminar, you will learn a breakthrough idea that will double your income and save you years of hard work.

When you invest 3 percent of your income back into yourself, year after year, you will eventually become one of the most skilled and highest paid professionals in your business. Regular investment in yourself and your skills will virtually guarantee your success.

I have countless friends around the country and throughout the world who started at the very bottom in selling and who are today earning hundreds of thousands of dollars per year as the result of continuous learning. And anything they have done, you can do as well.

ACTION EXERCISES

Develop an action plan for personal and professional development. Prepare a "training schedule" for yourself exactly as if you were training for a marathon or a big competition.

Become a "do-it-to-yourself project." Select the books you are going to read and block out time each day to read a specific number of pages. Determine the audio programs that can help you the most and begin listening to them. Resolve to attend one sales seminar every three months and discipline yourself to stick to your plan.

Dedicate yourself to lifelong learning. School is never out for the professional. The race is on, and you are in it. Be sure that you do everything you have to do, in terms of preparation, to win. Never stop learning and growing in your field.

Accept Complete Responsibility for Results

Hold yourself responsible for a
higher standard than anybody else
expects of you. Never excuse yourself.

—HENRY WARD BEECHER

Sometimes I will begin a sales seminar by asking, "How many people here are self-employed?"

Usually, about 15 to 20 percent of the hands go up. I then stop and ask a confident-looking person in the audience, "How many people here would you say are self-employed?"

He or she almost always replies, in a loud voice, "We all are!"

I then say, "You're right! The biggest mistake you can ever make is to think that you work for anyone else but yourself. We are all self-employed."

The highest paid sales professionals in every field accept 100 percent responsibility for their lives and for everything that happens to them. They see themselves as the presidents of their own professional sales corporations. They view themselves as self-employed.

They say, "If it's to be, it's up to me." They refuse to make excuses or to blame anyone else for anything in their lives that they are not happy about. If they don't like something, they know that it is up to them to get busy and change it. They accept complete responsibility and they refuse to complain or criticize.

The wonderful discovery is that the more responsibility you accept, the more you like and respect yourself. And the more you like and respect yourself, the more optimistic and positive you become. The more positive you are, the more creative and constructive you feel. As you accept more responsibility, you become more personally powerful and irresistible. You feel terrific about yourself. And the better you feel, the more you sell. Eventually, you reach the point where you feel unstoppable, like a force of nature.

The foundation of a healthy personality is the complete acceptance of personal responsibility for your life and for everything that happens to you. From now on, see yourself as the president of an entrepreneurial company with one employee—yourself. See yourself as responsible for selling your product—

your personal services—into a competitive market-place. Look upon your employer as your best client. See yourself as the boss of your own life.

As the president of your own professional sales corporation, you are paid for *results,* not activities. If you want more money, make more sales. In the long run, you determine your own income by what you do and by what you neglect to do.

Do you want to increase your income? Then go to the nearest mirror and negotiate with your "boss." The person in the mirror makes the decisions that determine the course of your life.

Here is an exercise for you: Make out a check to yourself on the first of the month for the amount you want to earn that month. Then, for the rest of the month, figure out how you are going to make payroll. You're the boss. It's your company. It's your life.

This is how the highest paid salespeople think about themselves and their work. When you practice thinking, all day long, the way that the top people think, you will eventually do the same things and get the same results that the top people get. You will begin to take complete control over every part of your career and your personal life. You will move onto the fast track and start to become a sales superstar.

ACTION EXERCISES

Imagine that you are starting a new business called "You, Inc." Prepare a complete strategic plan for your business, starting with sales projections on a monthly, quarterly, and annual basis.

Develop a step-by-step series of goals and activities that you are going to engage in every day to reach your sales goals. Organize your life around the achievement of these goals, and refuse to accept or allow excuses for nonperformance.

Develop your own plans for marketing, sales, production, quality control, training and development, and finances. Accept complete responsibility for yourself and for everything that happens to you.

Become Brilliant
on the Basics

The quality of a person's life is
determined more by their commitment
to excellence than by any other
factor, no matter what the
external circumstances.

—VINCE LOMBARDI

On many occasions, when we have offered our sales training programs to companies, we have been told, "We don't need that kind of training around here. All our people have years of experience."

We have a simple response to this objection. We say, "That's fine. Let's just give a simple test on selling basics to the members of your sales team. Everyone who passes the test doesn't need to take additional training."

What we have found is that virtually no one ever passes. Very few people are familiar enough even with the basics of selling to pass a simple multiple-choice exam. This means that salespeople who are already doing well could probably be selling far more if they were trained better on the basics. Salespeople who have never been trained at all can change their lives.

The AIDA Model of Selling

The AIDA Model describes the basic sales process. It has been used consistently throughout history. The four letters in AIDA stand for "Attention, Interest, Desire, and Action," the logical process of making a buying decision. Whenever you are having problems in your sales, it is because you are falling down in one of these four areas.

Get the Prospect to Listen to You

The first word, "Attention," requires that before you begin selling to anyone, you must break his or her pre-occupation. You must get the customer to listen to you and pay attention to you. The fact is that everyone is busy today. Therefore, every sales call is an interruption of something else that the customer is doing.

To get a customer's attention, you must ask a question or present an idea aimed at a specific benefit that the customer wants or a specific need of the customer that your product or service can fulfill. You must answer the first question of every prospect in your opening communication, which is, Why should I listen to you?

For example, in selling to a business customer, you could ask, "Would you like to see an idea that could save you time or money in your current operations?"

This question goes right to the heart of the concerns of almost every businessperson and tells the prospect why it might be of benefit to listen to you. If the prospect has a need to save time or money, this question will get his or her attention.

Whatever you sell, you can design a question or statement that will attract the attention of a prospect. Your question should focus on a specific desire of the prospect to achieve, avoid, or preserve something. For example, one of the most successful ads in the world, for Preparation H, is the word "Hemorrhoids?" It is simple and immediately catches the attention of qualified prospects.

Get the Prospect Interested

The second letter in the AIDA Model stands for "Interest." You arouse interest by showing features of your product or service or by explaining how your product or service can improve the life or work of the prospect.

A product demonstration arouses interest. A presentation of your services, showing how they can improve the prospect's work or business, maintains interest.

People are curious. They are interested in knowing about new products and services. But interest is not enough. The presentation or demonstration must connect with a need or desire or no purchase will take place.

Arouse Buying Desire

The third letter in the AIDA Model stands for "Desire." This is the part of the sales presentation where you explain the benefits that the prospect will enjoy from using your product or service. *Features* arouse interest, but *desire* causes the prospect to buy. If your prospect says something like "I want to think it over," what he or she is really saying is "You have not aroused my buying desire high enough for me to want to proceed at this time."

Your ability to think through and determine the real benefits that will motivate a prospective customer to buy is the most important part of selling. Your job is then to find prospects who intensely desire these benefits.

Some benefits that are most likely to stimulate buying desire are

1. Saving or making money
2. Saving or gaining time or increasing convenience

3. Being healthy, secure, popular, respected, or current
4. Improving one's personal or business situation in some way

Your primary job is to determine the key buying desire that your product or service can arouse in the mind and emotions of a particular prospect and then to convince him or her overwhelmingly that he or she will have that desire fulfilled with what you are selling.

Closing the Sale

The last letter in the AIDA Model stands for "Action." This is the part of the process where you ask the customer to make a definite buying decision, to take action on your offer. This is where you close the sale.

Later in this book, I will give you some proven techniques to get the customer to take action on your offer. For now, it is essential that you are clear about the AIDA Model and that you follow the steps in the correct order.

It is amazing how many salespeople mix up these four parts of the sale, getting them out of order, jumping back and forth from one to the other, or omitting them altogether. But they are like numbers in a sequence to open a lock. If they are out of order, they won't work at all, even if they are the correct numbers.

For you to be a top salesperson, you must become an expert in all four areas. You must learn and practice each phase of the sale until you reach the point where you can do all of them easily and automatically.

ACTION EXERCISES

Write each of the words in the AIDA Model at the top of separate sheets of paper. Then, write ten statements that you can use to connect better with your prospect in each area.

Give yourself a grade on a scale of one to ten in each area to assess how well you are doing today. Ask your colleagues and your sales manager to grade you as well. Go to work on the skill area that can help you the most.

Develop an opening question or positioning statement that grabs the prospect's attention and makes him or her want to listen to you. If necessary, rephrase your introductory question or statement so that a qualified prospect would respond with immediate interest.

Identify the key benefits that a customer will enjoy from owning or using what you sell. Which are the most important? Create a single sentence that summarizes the important benefits and repeat it often.

Build Long-Term Relationships

Fully 85 percent of the happiness

and success you enjoy in life will be

determined by the quality of your

relationships with others.

—BRIAN TRACY

All of your selling success today, and for the rest of your career, will be based on the quality of the relationships that you form with your customers. Because of the complexity of your product or service, customers are usually unable to make an accurate judgment on the details of what you are selling. Instead, they have to depend upon how they feel about you and your claims. For most customers today, the relationship comes first. It is more important than the product or service itself.

More than twenty years of research and millions of dollars have been spent by Neil Rackham and

Huthwaite Associates interviewing more than 55,000 customers before and after a sale or nonsale. One of the conclusions of their data is that the bigger the sale and the longer the life of the product or service are, the more important the relationship is in making the sale.

The building and maintaining of high-quality sales relationships proceeds in four stages. We call this the Relationship Selling Model. The first stage, roughly 40 percent of the sale, is the development of trust. This is best achieved by asking good questions and listening closely to the answers. In fact, a recent survey of the members of the Purchasing Managers Association of America (PMAA) concluded that the salespeople these professional buyers rated "the best" were the people who asked the most questions before attempting to sell.

The second stage of building high-quality sales relationships, 30 percent of the process, is focusing on identifying the true needs and wants of the prospect. Instead of talking about what you are selling, you ask questions about the prospect and his or her situation. You probe the answers you get and, as Stephen Covey says, "Seek first to understand, then to be understood."

Once you have built a high level of trust by asking questions and seeking to understand how your product or service can help the prospect in some way, you move to phase three, 20 percent of the Relationship Selling Model, which is *presenting solutions*. In this stage, you show the prospect how he or she could be better off with what you are selling than he or she is today. You carefully match the prospect's expressed needs with the specific features and benefits of your product or service.

In phase four, the final 10 percent of the Relationship Selling Model, you ask for confirmation from the prospect that what you are offering and what he or she needs are the same. You ask the prospect to make a decision and take action on your offering. You close the sale.

The Relationship Selling Model is based on trust. You develop trust by asking the customer about his or her needs and then by listening intently to the answers. The more you ask good questions and listen carefully to the customer, the more the customer will trust you and open up to you. When the customer trusts you enough, he or she will tell you everything you need to know to either make a sale or to determine that this customer is not a good prospect for what you are selling.

The very best salespeople are "relationship experts." They focus all of their attention on the relationship before they begin talking about their products or services. And as a result, they sell far more than the average salesperson. They get far more resales and referrals. They eventually move to the top of their fields.

ACTION EXERCISES

Focus first and foremost on the prospect and the relationship—before anything else. Concentrate on building a high level of trust. Only when you have built a bridge of understanding of the prospect's real needs should you start talking about what you are selling. When the relationship is strong, the sale will take care of itself.

Develop a series of questions aimed at fully understanding the customer and his or her situation. Ask your questions in a logical sequence, from the general to the particular. You can even make a list of these questions and give it to the prospect at the beginning of your meeting. (See chapter 5.) Then go through the list together to assure a high level of understanding between you before you begin your product or service presentation.

Be a Financial Improvement Specialist

A single idea—the sudden flash of an idea—may be worth a million dollars.

—Robert Collier

In consultative selling, you position yourself as a consultant, an expert, an advisor, a helper, and a teacher in the sales situation. Above all, you position yourself as a problem solver. You ask good questions and listen attentively to the answers.

When you are selling to businesses especially, you should position yourself as a "financial improvement specialist." This requires that you focus all your attention on showing the customer how his or her business can be financially better off as the result of using your product or service.

Customers of top salespeople describe these salespeople as consultants, "unpaid members of my own staff." They say, "He/she really understands my situation." This must be your aim as well.

Begin the sales process by asking questions about your prospect's business, seeking to understand how sales and revenues are generated, how costs and expenses are incurred, and how profits are made. Put yourself in the position of the business owner or executive and try to see yourself as being personally involved in achieving the financial results for which he or she is responsible.

Once you understand how your prospect's business or department operates, then find a way to define what you sell in *financial* terms. Your primary aim is to demonstrate to the prospect that the financial benefit of dealing with you is greater than the cost of what you are selling.

Many companies use "internal rate of return" to evaluate a new business expenditure. This is the return on investment that they aim to attain in purchasing new equipment of any kind. For example, a company may set 15 percent as its "IRR." This means that for you to sell the company something, you must demonstrate that it will save or make the company 15 percent or more each year and eventually pay for itself.

The higher the rate of return that a business can achieve in using your product or service, the more attractive it is to buy and use because it basically pays for itself and yields a profit.

The most important decision criterion business-people use in evaluating a prospective purchase or expenditure is called "time to payback." This is the amount of time that will pass before the company gets 100 percent of its money back. This is determined by dividing the IRR into the number 72. (For example, if your product or service will save or earn the company 20 percent of its cost each year, the time to payback is 3.6 years.) The company then compares this rate of return against alternate uses of the same money.

In determining time to payback, the prospect has four key questions, spoken or unspoken, that you must answer. The first question is, How much does it cost?

The second question you must answer in your presentation is, How much do I get back in return for my investment?

The third question is, How fast do I get this amount back?

The fourth question is, How sure can I be that what you say is true?

The greater the clarity with which you can answer these questions, the easier it is for the prospect to buy from you. The fuzzier you are in answering these questions, the harder it is for the customer to buy from you. If neither you nor the customer can figure out the rate and speed of return, no sale will take place.

As a financial improvement specialist, continually demonstrate and prove how the customer can achieve more of his or her business goals as the result of following your advice and recommendations. Position yourself as an unpaid member of the customer's staff, helping him or her to increase sales, reduce costs, or boost profits. Show that your product or service is actually "free" in that the customer ultimately gets back far more in dollar terms than he or she pays in the first place. This is a vital key to high-level selling.

ACTION EXERCISES

Determine the exact rate of return, in terms of time or money saved or gained from using what you sell. Describe your product or service in terms of how it affects the financial situation of your prospective customer. Think in terms of the direct as well as the indirect financial benefits your customer will enjoy as a result of using your product or service.

Identify the prospects in your market who can most profit from the financial benefits your product or service can contribute. Focus more of your selling energies on those prospects who can profit the most rapidly from what you sell. Build your sales activities around finding more and more of these prime prospects. Focus continually on "time to payback."

Use Educational Selling with Every Customer

Nature understands no jesting. She is always true, always serious, always severe: she is always right, and the errors and faults are always those of man.

—JOHANN WOLFGANG VON GOETHE

A major reason that prospects do not buy is because they do not fully understand what you are selling and how they can use and benefit from it. Many salespeople assume that after one sales presentation, the prospect is as familiar with the details of the product or service as they are. This can be a big mistake.

When I was selling participations in real estate investments to senior executives, I falsely assumed that these captains of industry, with hundreds and sometimes thousands of staff, were as knowledgeable

about real estate as they were about their own businesses. As a result, I would often breeze through the
details of my product and expect them to understand
the full range of benefits and advantages of what I
was offering.

It didn't take me too many lost sales to realize that
I had to explain my product in careful detail, exactly
as if I was teaching a new subject to a new student, if
I wanted to sell it. This was my introduction to the
importance of positioning myself as a *teacher* in the
sales process.

In educational selling, you take a low-pressure/
no-pressure approach. You do not try to influence or
persuade the customer in any way. You ask good questions and listen closely to the answers. You lean forward and take notes. You position yourself as a teacher
and as a helper rather than as a salesperson. The best
way to do this is to use the "Show, Tell, and Ask Questions" Method of presenting your product or service.

Show the Customer

In the "show" part of the presentation, explain or
demonstrate how your product or service works to
achieve a particular result or benefit. Get the prospect
involved. Ask him or her to do something, try something out personally, or make calculations to prove
your points.

Tell the Customer

In the "tell" part of the educational selling process, explain the features and benefits of your product or service, using stories, statistics, research results, and anecdotes from other satisfied customers. Like a lawyer, "build a case" for what you are selling, presenting evidence in the form of visual aids or written materials that "prove" the quality and usefulness of your product.

Ask the Customer

In the "ask questions" phase, pause regularly to ask questions and invite feedback on what you have presented so far. One mark of top salespeople is that they keep their prospects involved in the sales conversation by continually requesting comments and opinions as they go along. Poor salespeople are often so nervous that they race through their product descriptions without giving the prospect an opportunity to question or object.

Here is a simple model you can adapt to your own product:

> "Because of this _____ (product feature),
> you can _____ (product benefit), which
> means _____ (customer benefit)."

For example, imagine you were selling a new office computer. You could say, "Because of this Pentium III microprocessor (product feature), you can run multiple programs simultaneously (product benefit), which means that you can get far more work done in a shorter period of time (customer benefit)."

When you "show, tell, and ask questions," you position yourself as an educator rather than as a salesperson. By asking questions, you learn how your customer can be better off by using what you are selling. Your "lesson plan" consists of teaching the customer how he or she can best use your product or service and benefit from it in his or her life and work. With many products, especially technical products with many capabilities, you can build tremendous perceived value by teaching the customer all the different ways that he or she can use your product or service to get even greater results and enjoyment.

The more competent you become at learning your prospect's real needs, and the better you teach your customer how to get the very most out of what you sell, the more the customer will like you, trust you, and want to do business with you, over and over again.

ACTION EXERCISES

Take out a sheet of paper and draw three lines down the page, creating three equal columns. At the top of each column, write the words "Product Feature," "Product Benefit," or "Customer Benefit."

List each positive sales feature of your product or service in the first column. In the second column, write the product benefit attached to each product feature. In the third column, define the customer benefit, the answer to the question, What's in it for me?

Practice positioning yourself as a "teacher" with your prospects. Focus your presentation on helping your prospect to understand how helpful your product or service can be, trusting fully that if he or she understands completely, the sale will take place automatically.

Build
Megacredibility
with Every
Prospect

Honesty is the first chapter
of the book of wisdom.

—THOMAS JEFFERSON

Fully 80 percent of the reason that qualified prospects do not buy a product or service is because they are afraid of making a mistake. As the result of countless negative buying experiences, starting in early childhood, we all have bought something and regretted it afterward. Perhaps we later learned that we had paid too much, had gotten the wrong product for our needs, were unable to get the product serviced or repaired, or had been outright lied to by the salesperson or company.

Because of this accumulated baggage of unhappy purchase decisions, prospective customers are usually suspicious, skeptical, and distrustful of sales offers, even when they want and need a particular product or service. And the larger and more expensive it is, the more cautious and doubtful they are.

Four factors exacerbate this hesitancy with any sales offer. The first is the *size* of the purchase. The more it costs, the more of a risk the prospect perceives in buying it.

The second risk factor is the *length of life* of the product. If it is meant to last for three or more years—and once it is purchased, it would be too expensive to buy another—the customer will naturally be hesitant to make a buying decision. The risk of making a mistake and being stuck with the wrong product is great.

The third risk factor is the *number of people* involved. Everyone has had the experience of making a buying decision and then being criticized for it by other people. Sometimes, they just complain about the choice. At other times, they point out how bad a decision it was considering other products or services available. The worst of all is when the decision turns out so badly that the buyer's position in his or her company is threatened. That is why IBM's most famous advertisement is "No one ever got fired for choosing IBM!"

The fourth risk factor is whether or not the purchaser is a *first-time buyer.* Has the customer ever bought or used this particular product or service? Has he or she ever bought it from you or your company? In either case, if the answer is no, the perceived risk is much higher.

The antidote to this natural and normal skepticism and lack of trust or confidence in any sales offer is *credibility*. The solution is to build up the customer's concept of you as a completely believable person selling a totally trustworthy product. Credibility is the core issue in any purchase decision. But credibility alone is not enough.

Today, it takes credibility for you just to get an appointment with a customer. But it takes *megacredibility* for you to get the sale. Megacredibility is defined as credibility that is far above and beyond an appeal to quality and service. It is credibility that is far greater than anything your competitors might be offering at the same time.

Megacredibility is an idea or feeling that can be, and must be, created in the heart and mind of the prospect. It is the critical intangible factor that underlies all successful sales efforts. Megacredibility is the outstanding quality of high-performing salespeople. And fortunately, megacredibility is something you can build, step by step, in every interaction with the customer.

There are five keys to building megacredibility. Each is vitally important. Each can determine the sale, depending upon whether you capitalize on it or not. And ignorance of these key factors is no excuse.

You Are the Key to the Sale

The first form of megacredibility is the credibility of the salesperson, *yourself.* Your personal credibility is so important that your appearance and your personality alone can make or break the sale.

Personal megacredibility has four parts: dress, grooming, accessories, and attitude. Each of these ingredients is essential. A deficiency in any one of these areas can be enough to cost you the sale.

Dress for Success

Customers are very visual. They seek clues from the way you look to determine how trustworthy and competent you are, and through your appearance they judge the trustworthiness and capabilities of your product, service, and company. Fully 95 percent of the first impression you make on a customer will be made by your clothes. This is because your clothes cover 95 percent of your body. For this reason, top salespeople "dress for success" on every occasion and with every customer. They leave nothing to chance.

Follow the leaders, not the followers. Look at the top salespeople in your field and then dress the way they do. As a general rule, you should spend twice as much on your clothes as you do now and buy half as many. You will like these good clothes so much that you will wear them more often, get more use and value from them, and feel better and more confident every time you put them on.

You should read at least one book on the subject of dressing for success in business. Don't believe any of what you hear about the "new" acceptability of casual dress. You don't ever want to find yourself selling against a competitor who looks a whole lot better than you do. Dress well when you visit customers. Make sure that you look like the kind of person a customer would be comfortable taking advice from.

Use your best judgment to determine the most appropriate dress for you in selling to your customers in your market. What is most acceptable changes by industry and region. For example, you would dress differently if you were to call on bankers or senior executives than you would if you were selling backhoes or grain driers to builders or farmers.

Look the Part

Your grooming is also important in determining the impression you make on your prospect, from the first meeting onward. The highest paid salespeople in almost every field tend to groom themselves in a conservative and understated way. Look at the pictures of the businesspeople in the "appointments" section of your local newspaper. They are always professional and businesslike, competent and believable in appearance. You should be as well.

The simplest rule about good dress and grooming is that nothing should distract the customer from your face, your person, and your conversation. The customer should get an impression of a professional salesperson without being conscious of a specific article of clothing or element of your grooming.

Accessories Can Help You or Hurt You

The correct accessories blend well with your clothes and your overall appearance. They enhance your overall "look" without drawing attention. They are the appropriate color, design, and texture to add to your overall impression of professionalism. Look at yourself in a mirror before you head out to a sales call, and solicit the opinions of others.

A Positive Mental Attitude

The fourth part of the initial impression you make on the prospect is your attitude. As a rule, you should always be positive, friendly, optimistic, and cheerful when you are selling. Customers prefer to deal with *nice* people, people who seem helpful and open. If you have personal problems, leave them at home or keep them to yourself. Be a pleasant, easygoing person to do business with.

Your Most Valuable Asset

The second part of megacredibility is the *reputation* of your company. According to Theodore Leavitt of Harvard Business School, a company's most valuable asset is "how it is *known* to its customers." This reputation is made up of many factors that customers experience in dealing with the company.

Fully 85 percent of sales made today are based on "word of mouth." This consists of what other people say about your product and your services. It is how your company is thought of and talked about by customers and noncustomers in the marketplace. The better your reputation, the lower the perceived risk in buying from you. The more other customers speak well of you, the easier it is for new customers to accept your recommendations to go ahead with the purchase.

Get It on Paper

The third part of megacredibility is *testimonials.* These consist of letters, lists, photographs, and other third-party statements. All build confidence and lower the fear of making a buying mistake.

One good letter from a satisfied customer may be all you need to convince a prospect that he or she is safe in buying from you. Make it a point to ask for a testimonial letter each time you get a positive comment from a customer. Carry the letters with you in plastic sleeves in a three-ring binder. They are incredibly powerful in building megacredibility.

If you can, make a list of the people or companies that have bought from you. The longer the list or the better known the customers, the more powerful it is in building confidence.

Another form of credibility is photographs or videos of happy customers. A picture is worth a thousand words when it comes to overcoming skepticism and building megacredibility in a sales conversation. Often people will not buy a product or service until they know who else has bought it and been happy with it. Be sure to volunteer this information clearly in your sales conversation.

Put Your Best Foot Forward

The fourth part of megacredibility is the *presentation*. A well-thought-out, completely professional, customer-focused presentation adds value to the product or service and actually increases the price you can charge for it. A planned and prepared presentation builds your credibility to a high level. This credibility may be all you need to overcome the fear and misgivings that hold most customers back.

An excellent presentation is one where you match your product or service to the needs of the customer, exactly as the customer has told them to you in the questioning and listening part of the sales conversation. You show the customer that the exact benefits he or she wants are contained in what you sell. You avoid talking about things the customer has not expressed an interest in buying.

Emphasize the Value

The fifth ingredient of megacredibility is the *product* or *service* itself. Your presentation should demonstrate clearly that the product you offer is the ideal solution to the customer's needs and that the value of what you sell greatly outweighs the price you are asking.

The customer must be convinced that, all things considered, he or she will be better off with what you are selling than he or she would be with a competitive product or with the money that it costs.

Here is the great rule for sales success: "Everything counts."

Everything counts! Everything you do in a sales situation either helps or hurts. It either moves you toward the sale or moves you away. It is either increasing your credibility or decreasing your credibility. But nothing is neutral. Everything counts. All top professionals know that everything counts. They leave nothing to chance. Neither should you.

ACTION EXERCISES

Make a list of the five ingredients of mega-credibility. Determine one thing you could do in each area to increase your believability and lower the prospect's perception of risk.

Begin with your clothes, your grooming, and your overall appearance. Imagine that there is a contest for making a great first impression on a prospective customer. Would you win? If not, decide today what you are going to change and improve so that you will look more convincing when you meet your next prospect.

Review your sales materials and your presentation. Determine what you could do immediately to build the credibility of your company and your product. Make greater use of testimonials and visuals during your presentation. Use any method you can to demonstrate that what you are selling is more valuable and desirable than the price you are asking and that *your* product or service is superior to any competitive product or service.

Handle Objections Effectively

It is the constant and determined effort that breaks down all resistance, sweeps away all obstacles.

—CLAUDE BRISTOL

Every prospect has questions and concerns about your offering that must be dealt with effectively before he or she can proceed with confidence. This is normal and natural and to be expected. Your ability to answer objections effectively is a critical skill that will largely determine your level of sales and income. Your job is to master this skill.

When I began selling and the prospect objected to my offer, I would be crushed. When the prospect said things like, "I can't afford it," "We're not in the market for that right now," "We don't need what you are selling," "Your price is too high," or "We can get it cheaper somewhere else," I would accept the objection without arguing and go on to the next prospect.

Then I learned that objections are simply part of a normal sales process. They are inevitable and unavoidable. My job was to identify the major objections that I would get and then develop answers to them.

The fact is that objections are good. Objections indicate *interest*. Videotapes of thousands of sales calls show that successful sales have twice as many objections as unsuccessful sales. When the prospect starts objecting, it means that he or she is beginning to consider your offer seriously. You now have a chance to sell.

The Law of Six applies to objections. This law says that there are never more than six major objections to any offer. Your job is to sort each possible objection into one of the six categories and then to develop a bulletproof answer to that objection.

The objections could revolve around your price, the customer's satisfaction with his or her existing supplier, complacency with the existing situation, the newness of or lack of familiarity with your product, or even knee jerk sales resistance that comes automatically.

The Sweep-Aside Method

When you experience initial sales resistance to any offer such as when prospects say, "I'm not interested" or "I can't afford it," you can reply to these objections with the Sweep-Aside Method. Say these words positively and politely: "That's all right. Most people in your situation felt the same way when I first called on them. But now they've become our best customers and they recommend us to their friends."

With a qualified prospect, this usually triggers the response, *"What is it?"* to which you respond, "That's exactly what I would like to talk to you about, and I only need a few minutes of your time."

The first rule in handling objections effectively is that you should hear them out completely, without interrupting. Even when the prospect is objecting, you are getting an opportunity to listen, and *listening builds trust.* A negative prospect can be transformed into a neutral or positive prospect when you practice the "white magic" of attentive listening.

Treat each objection as if it were actually a question. When the prospect says, "I can't afford it," say, "That's a good question! How can you justify the price at this time? Let me see if I can answer that for you."

Here are three responses you can use for any objection:

First, you can pause, smile, and then ask, "How do you mean?" This question is almost impossible not to answer. You can use it over and over again in the sales conversation. "How do you mean?" or "How do you mean, exactly?"

Second, you can say, "Obviously you have a good reason for saying that. Do you mind if I ask what it is?" Often the customer does not have a good reason for objecting, and this response will help to clarify that.

The third way you can handle objections is by using the "Feel, Felt, Found" Method. When a customer says something like "It costs too much," you can say, "I understand exactly how you *feel*. Others *felt* the same way when they first heard the price. But this is what they *found* when they began using our product or service."

Then go on to explain how other customers found that the benefit or value of your product more than justified the price you were charging. Demonstrate that what the customer receives is greatly in excess of the added cost that he or she has to pay. Show how happy other customers were afterward, even though they spent more than they initially expected.

When I do sales consulting with a company, I explain that salespeople can increase their sales in two ways. First, they can present more benefits and reasons to buy. Second, they can effectively remove more of the objections, or reasons not to buy, that are holding their prospects back.

We then conduct a sentence-completion exercise to identify the main obstacles in customers' minds that hold them back from buying. We complete the sentence, "I could sell to every qualified prospect I spoke to if he or she just didn't say _____."

We go around the room and write out, on flip charts, every single objection that anyone has ever received. We then "cluster" these objections into their logical categories, which are never more than six. Finally, we go around the room once more and solicit the very best answers that anyone has discovered for answering each particular category of objection.

Once you arm yourself with a repertoire of excellent answers, you will sell with greater confidence and effectiveness in any market. Objections will never hold you back again.

ACTION EXERCISES

Make a list of every reason that prospects give you for not buying what you are selling. Organize this list by priority and frequency. Determine the major objections you get that stop you from making sales to qualified prospects.

Write these objections on the left-hand side of a sheet of paper. Draw a line down the middle. Then write a logical and persuasive answer to each objection in the right-hand column.

(continued)

Ask other salespeople how they answer these objections. Practice responding naturally to them when someone brings them up. Get testimonial letters or other proof to demonstrate that the objection is not a valid reason not to buy. From now on, refuse to take no for an answer unless there is a very good reason that makes it impossible for the prospect to buy.

Deal with Price Professionally

Men who accomplish great things
in the industrial world are those
who have faith in the money
producing power of their ideas.

—CHARLES FILLMORE

Price is seldom the reason for buying or not buying anything. Sometimes I ask my sales audiences if they would like me to prove this claim. I then ask them, perhaps one thousand participants, "Is there a single person in this room who has a single item about their person that they bought *solely* because it was the cheapest available?"

No one ever raises his or her hand. The point is clear. Many factors go into the buying decision, and of course price is one of them. But price is never the main reason. The main reason is always something else. Your job is to find it and deal with that concern effectively.

According to one study at Harvard, fully 94 percent of sales in America are made on a nonprice basis. Follow-up surveys with customers who argued and negotiated long and hard over price turned up the surprising fact that they finally made their decision on nonprice factors. Factors such as suitability, convenience, reputation of the company or product, service, appearance, and appropriateness to the customer were more important.

The first rule in dealing with price objections is never to argue or defend your prices. Instead, probe gently and professionally to find out the real reason that the customer is hesitating. Ask, "How do you mean?" Use the "Feel, Felt, Found" Method described in chapter 13. Position yourself as a consultant and ask good questions to uncover the real needs of the customer. Focus on the value of what you are selling rather than getting into a price argument.

In addition, you can deal with price in several special ways: First, when the prospect says, "Your price is too high," reply by politely asking, "Why do you say that?"

Remember that *the person who asks questions has control.* When you ask a question, you must pause and remain perfectly silent until the prospect replies. Then, whenever possible, follow with another question and again remain silent while the prospect answers. This method is vastly more effective than talking and attempting to overwhelm the prospect with features, benefits, facts, and figures.

Second, when the prospect says, "I can't afford it," gently ask, "Why do you *feel* that way?" Then remain silent as you lean forward attentively, waiting for an answer.

Prospects often have no answers to these questions. However, by asking them, not only will you maintain control over the flow of the sales conversation, you will often learn the real reason behind a prospect's hesitation.

Here is another key rule with regard to price: *Price out of place kills the sale.* If you get into a price discussion before the prospect thoroughly understands what you are selling and the benefits to him or her of owning and using it, you will usually kill all possibilities of a sale. You must therefore put off the discussion of price until the customer has indicated that he or she likes and wants what you are selling.

Often the prospect will say near the beginning of a sales call, "Just tell me how much it is and I'll tell you if I'm interested."

If you give in to the temptation to give the price at this time, you will usually find yourself back on the street in a few minutes, wondering what happened. Instead, say, "I know price is important to you. Could I come back to that a little later, after I've had a chance to understand your current situation?"

Sometimes, prospects will be quite demanding and will insist that you state the price before allowing you to proceed. When I was faced this situation, I would simply counter by saying, "I don't know."

"What do you mean, 'You don't know?'" the prospect would ask. I would then say, "I don't even know if what we have would be suitable for you. But if I could ask you a couple of questions, I could give you an estimate that would be accurate to within a couple of dollars. For example, I would need to know what you are doing now in this area."

Once you postpone the price discussion, you can then go into a questioning process, positioning yourself as a consultant, focusing on uncovering the problem or need of the prospect for which your product or service is the ideal solution.

The third way to handle a price objection is this: When the prospect says, "That's more than I expected to pay," respond by asking, "How far apart are we?"

Often, the prospect has a price in mind that he or she thinks is the amount your product should cost. Sometimes, the prospect has budgeted a certain amount to purchase what you are selling. Once you discover that number, as long as it is reasonably close to what you are asking, your job is to demonstrate that the difference in price is more than made up for by the increase in value that he or she will receive.

Never be hesitant to reassure the prospect that "This is a very good price" or "This is a great deal; it is worth every penny you pay." Or you can say, "This is an excellent product or service; you will be very happy with it."

Customers today do not want the lowest price. They have had enough experience with low-price items to know that they are also low-quality items and usually cause far more problems than they cure. Instead, customers want a "good price," a "fair price," a "good deal," a "great deal." But they don't want something just because it is cheap.

The fourth way to handle price is used when the customer opens with the question, "How much is it?" He or she demands to know the price even before you have had a chance to ask any questions or before the customer even knows what you are selling. At this moment, you are in great and immediate danger of losing both the prospect and the sale. If you answer this question by giving the price, you will invariably get the response "I can't afford it!" and the conversation will be over.

Here is a direct, "in your face" reply to the question, "How much is it?" You smile, even into the phone, and say, "That's the best part! If it's not exactly right for you, there's no charge."

This almost always brings the prospect to a halt. "No charge?" he or she will say, "What do you mean?"

You then say, "If whatever I'm selling is not exactly right for you, you're not going to take it, are you?"

The prospect will say, "No, I'm not!"

You then say, "And if you don't take it, then there's no charge, right?"

The prospect will then say, "That's true. What is it, then?"

You reply, "That's exactly what I want to talk to you about, and I just need a few minutes of your time. I've got something I have to show you." You then proceed to arrange a face-to-face appointment and you are on your way.

The key to dealing with price objections professionally is for you to be proud of your prices. Remember that they have been carefully set on the basis of many factors. They are fair and reasonable. The value that the customer gets is far greater than the amount he or she pays. By helping the prospect to buy your product or service at these prices, you are doing him or her a favor. You are helping to improve the quality of his or her life or work.

ACTION EXERCISES

Make a list of all the benefits that customers will enjoy from owning and using your product or service. Wherever possible, quantify these benefits in terms of the dollar value they represent. Build your sales presentation around these values and emphasize what the customer gets versus what he or she pays.

Make a list of all the price objections you receive from your prospects and then develop positive responses to each one. Ask your colleagues how they deal with specific price concerns. Practice these answers at every opportunity.

Finally, if you are stopped or stumped by a price objection, ask the prospect, "Let's put price aside for a moment. Is there any other reason why you would hesitate buying my product or service right now?" This question often brings out the real reason behind the prospect's reluctance to buy.

Know How to Close the Sale

Our grand business is not to see

what lies dimly at a distance,

but to do what lies clearly at hand.

—THOMAS CARLYLE

Your ability to ask for the order at the end of the presentation or at the end of the sales process is absolutely essential to your success. Fortunately, tens of thousands of sales conversations have been video-taped so we now know exactly how the highest paid salespeople close sales most of the time.

The sales process follows a logical series of steps from beginning to end. First, you establish rapport and trust with the prospect to assure that he or she likes you and is open to following your advice.

Second, you ask questions to clearly identify what the prospect needs and wants in the area in which you sell.

Third, you show the prospect that what you are selling, all things considered, is the best possible solution for him or her at this time.

Fourth, you satisfactorily answer any objections or questions the prospect may have.

Finally, you ask the prospect to take action on your offering. This last step is the key determinant of your income.

Before you move to close the sale, you can ask one of these two questions: First, "Do you have any questions or concerns that I haven't covered so far?"

If the customer says no, you can then smile and confidently ask for the buying decision.

Second, you can ask, "Does this make sense to you so far?"

If the prospect says yes, you can then proceed to close the sale.

You can use three excellent techniques to ask for the order. The first method is the "Invitational Close." It is perhaps the simplest of all. When the prospect says that he or she has no more questions or concerns, you could ask, "Well then, why don't you give it a try?"

This is an amazingly effective closing technique. It is low-keyed, friendly, professional, and completely lacking in pressure of any kind.

If you are selling a service or you represent a large company, you could say, "Why don't you give us a try?"

If it is a tangible product, you could even say, "Why don't you take it?"

You can then reinforce these words by adding, "And I'll take care of all the details." Often a prospect doesn't know how much he or she wants what you are selling until you offer to take care of all the details.

The second technique you can use is called the "Directive Close." This is the most popular closing technique used by the highest paid salespeople in almost every industry.

With this technique you ask the question, "Does this make sense to you so far?"

When the prospect says yes, you say, "Well then, the next step is this" You then go on to describe the plan of action from this point forward. You explain what the prospect needs to do now and how much of a deposit you will require. You take out the order form or the contract and begin filling it out.

You proceed to wrap up the sale as if the prospect had just said, "I'll take it!" You then add, "And I'll take care of all the details."

This is a form of the "Assumption Close" or the "Selling Past the Sale Close," where you assume the sale, in advance, and carry on exactly as if the decision to buy had already been made. The strength of this closing technique is that it enables you to take and control the initiative. It keeps you in the driver's seat.

The third closing technique you can use is called the "Authorization Close." At the end of the sales conversation, you double-check to make sure that the prospect has no further questions. You then take out your order form, place a check mark by the signature line, push the order form across the desk, and say, "Well then, if you'll just authorize this, *we'll get started right away!*"

Sometimes the customer doesn't know how badly he or she wants what you're offering until you offer to get started "right away."

There are dozens of proven ways for you to close the sale, each of them appropriate for different situations. If you have built a solid relationship with the prospect, positioned yourself as a consultant and a teacher, and matched your product or service carefully to the real needs of your prospect, the close is relatively easy and painless.

But you must be prepared to ask for the sale. Fully 50 percent of all sales conversations end without the salesperson asking for the order or even for a subsequent meeting. Most sales are closed only after the fifth time the salesperson asks the prospect to make a buying decision. Your ability and willingness to ask for the prospect's business can be the deciding factor in your career.

The future belongs to the askers. Financial and personal success goes to those men and women who confidently and courageously ask for what they want, and if they don't get it, they ask again and again.

Of course, you should ask politely. Ask courteously. Ask expectantly. Ask in a friendly and persistent way. You should ask for appointments. Ask what customers are doing now and how satisfied they are with it. Ask about their future plans and needs. Ask who else they are considering. Ask for more information. Ask for references and referrals. But above all, ask for the business. Ask for the order. Never be afraid to ask for what you want. This is the key to success both in selling and in life.

◆ ───────────────────────────────

ACTION EXERCISES

Plan your closing in advance. Think through your sales process and presentation and be ready to ask a closing question as soon as you think your prospect is ready to make a buying decision.

Practice and memorize the closing techniques explained above. Read, study, listen to audio programs, and build your repertoire of closing techniques. The more confident you become about your ability to close, the
(continued)

more confident you will become in prospecting and presenting as well.

Remember that your job success depends on your ability to close the sale. Everything that you do up to that moment is preparation. Asking for the order is the key to the sales process, and your goal must be to become absolutely excellent in this area. Don't hesitate!

Make Every
Minute Count

Set priorities for your goals. A major
part of successful living lies in the ability
to put first things first. Indeed, the
reason most major goals are not
achieved is that we spend our time
doing second things first.

—ROBERT J. McKAIN

Your most valuable asset, in terms of cash flow, is your earning ability. It is your ability to go out each day and apply your skills in your profession to earn an excellent income. The most successful sales-people, in every field, work on maximizing their earning ability every single day.

It has taken you an entire lifetime of education and experience to develop your earning ability to where it is today. You should never take it for granted.

By leveraging your earning ability, you can enjoy one of the highest standards of living in the world by focusing your time and talents on selling more and more of your products or services in your marketplace.

Your most precious resource is your time—the minutes and hours of each day. It is all you really have to sell. In fact, your entire lifestyle today—your home, your car, your bank account, and so on—is the result of how you have traded your time up to now. If, for any reason, you are not completely happy with the results of the way you have *traded* your time in the past, you can begin right now to trade it better for the future.

One of the very best uses of your time is to increase your earning ability. One of the greatest timesavers of all is to get better at the most important things you do. Nothing else will give you a more rapid and predictable increase in your income and your standard of living. The more you invest your time and money back into yourself, into making yourself more capable and confident at the activities that pay you the most, the more you will earn and the happier you will be.

Resolve today to become an expert at time management. This one skill will make more things possible for you than perhaps any other, for without it, no other skills can be utilized to their fullest extent.

The core principle of time management is the ability to do *first things first;* to set priorities among competing demands on your time; and above all, to think, plan, decide, and then to take the appropriate action.

The most important word in setting priorities is "consequences." An activity is valuable in direct proportion to the potential consequences of doing it or not. The task that represents the most serious potential consequences is almost always the one with the highest priority.

There are four questions that you can ask and answer continually to keep yourself focused on your highest priorities. First, ask yourself, "What are *my highest value activities* in terms of the potential consequences of doing them or not doing them?"

For you, a sales professional, they are (1) prospecting, (2) establishing rapport, (3) identifying needs, (4) making presentations, (5) answering objections, (6) closing the sale, and (7) getting referrals from customers. Your competence in each of these areas, and in all of them together, determines your sales and your income. What is the most important activity you need to be engaging in right now?

Second, ask yourself, "Why am I on the payroll?"

Every minute of every day, you should imagine that your boss were traveling along with you, observing your actions, and preparing your annual performance appraisal. Keep asking yourself, "Is what I'm doing right now leading to a sale?" This result is the sole reason you are on the payroll. If what you are doing is not leading to a sale, stop doing it and start doing something that is.

The third question you can ask and answer repeatedly is, "What can I, and only I, do that, if done well, will make a significant contribution to my company and myself?"

This is a task, such as prospecting or closing sales, that only you can do. If you don't do it, it will not be done by someone else. The successful completion of this task, whatever it is, should be a major priority for you.

The fourth question for setting priorities, the best single question of all, is this: "What is the most valuable use of my time right now?"

There is only one answer to this question at any time. Your primary job is to identify the answer and then to work on this one task exclusively until it is complete.

Ask each of these questions of yourself continually. Hold your own feet to the fire. Discipline yourself to stay focused on those activities that can contribute the most to your success.

All highly effective people think clearly in two dimensions of time: long-term and short-term. First, they are very clear about their future goals and ambitions. Second, they are very focused in the moment in that they are always doing the one thing that can most contribute to achieving their most important goals. Your ability to hold these two thoughts simultaneously is the key to high productivity.

◆

ACTION EXERCISES

Begin today to plan every day, week, and month in advance. Use a time planner of some kind, either written or electronic. Any of these systems will help you get organized if you will discipline yourself to use them every day.

Perhaps the best time management tool of all is a list. Make a list of the next day's activities each evening. Go through the list and set priorities on the items. Determine which are more important and which are less important. Decide which activities can contribute the most to your life and which contribute the least.

Each morning, begin with your most important task and discipline yourself to stay at it until it is 100 percent complete. This one habit will do more to improve your results and your life than anything else.

Apply the 80/20 Rule to Everything

Nothing can add more power to
your life than concentrating all of your
energies on a limited set of targets.

—NIDO QUBEIN

In 1895 in Italy, an economist named Vilfredo
Pareto discovered a principle that has had an enormous impact on economics and business ever since.
He found that you could divide members of society
into the "vital few," the 20 percent of the population
who controlled 80 percent of the wealth, and the "trivial many," those who possessed only 20 percent of the
wealth.

This is now called the Pareto Principle, and it has
proven to be universally valid in virtually every study
of economic activity. We call it the 80/20 Rule, and
you can apply it to every area of selling.

The 80/20 Rule says that 20 percent of your activities will account for 80 percent of your results. If you have a list of ten things to do, two of those activities will be as valuable, if not more valuable, than the other eight. One of your chief responsibilities is to continually analyze your tasks to be sure that you are working on the top 20 percent.

In selling, 20 percent of your prospects will account for 80 percent of your customers, 20 percent of your customers will account for 80 percent of your sales, 20 percent of your products and services will account for 80 percent of your sales volume, and so on.

In business, 20 percent of your activities will account for 80 percent of your profits. In addition, 20 percent of your activities will account for 80 percent of your expenses, and the activities that represent 80 percent of your expenses may not be closely related to your most profitable activities. In the worst of cases, businesses find themselves spending most of their time and money in areas that are not profitable at all.

Some years ago, a major insurance company analyzed the sales and incomes of its many thousands of salespeople throughout the country. The analysts found that the 80/20 Rule held up: 20 percent of the salespeople were making 80 percent of the sales and 80 percent of the commissions.

Then they compared the incomes of the people in the top 20 percent to the incomes of those in the bottom 80 percent. They found that the average income of those in the top 20 percent was *sixteen times* the average income of those in the lower 80 percent!

They then looked at the top 20 percent of the salespeople in the upper 20 percent—that is, the top 4 percent of the sales force—and found that their income amounted to 80 percent of the income of the top 20 percent. Some of the people in the top 4 percent were earning as much as fifty times the income of the people in the bottom 80 percent!

When I learned the results of this study, I resolved that I was going to do whatever it took to get into the top 20 percent and move up from there. I then discovered two principles that changed my life. First, I found that it took just as much time to be in the top 20 percent as to be in the bottom 80 percent. It took just as many days, weeks, and months of work to succeed greatly as to get average results.

The second thing I discovered was that there was very little difference in talent or ability between the high performers and the low performers, except for the way they used their time. It turned out that the high performers had developed the habit of working primarily on the top 20 percent of their activities, and the lower performers had not.

What this means, quite simply, is that for you to succeed greatly, you must always be focusing your time and energy on the few activities, the 20 percent of tasks, that can make a real difference in your life. Your ability to keep this focus will eventually move you to the top of your field.

On the other hand, the *inability* to focus on the top 20 percent of sales activities is the primary reason for failure, frustration, and underachievement in the sales profession. Even if you are working hard, it will do you no good if you are accomplishing more and more tasks of little value in comparison with what else you could be doing with the same time and energy.

ACTION EXERCISES

Make a list every day, before you begin work. Organize your list on the basis of the 80/20 Rule. Select the one or two tasks that are potentially more valuable than any of the others. Start on the first task and stay with it until it is complete.

Use the ABC Method to sort out your prospects and customers before you begin work. Make a list of all your prospects. Place an "A" next to those who have the highest potential, the top 20 percent. Place a "B" next to those of middle potential and a "C" next to those of low potential.

Conduct the same exercise with your customers to determine how often you call back on them. Visit your "A" customers personally on a regular basis. Visit your "B" customers less often, and phone them between visits. Visit your "C" customers occasionally, using the telephone and mail to keep in touch.

Keep Your Sales Funnel Full

The power which resides in man

is new in nature, and none but he

knows what that is that he can do,

nor does he know until he has tried.

— RALPH WALDO EMERSON

Professional selling has three stages, which have been the same throughout history. They are *prospect, present,* and *follow up.* These three phases constitute the three parts of the "sales funnel."

If ever you are not satisfied with your results, you can analyze your performance in terms of these three basic activities. If your sales and your income are down, it is because you are not prospecting enough, presenting enough, or following up and closing enough. The way to increase your sales is usually for you to increase the quality or quantity of your activities in one or more of these areas.

Imagine this basic sales model as a funnel. At the top of the funnel, you put in prospects. You have to call on a certain number of people, or *suspects,* to get a certain number of prospects. This number varies depending on the market, your product or service, your individual skills in prospecting, advertising, and many other factors.

The second part of the sales funnel is presenting. There is a direct ratio between the number of people you call on initially and the number of people who will agree to meet with you. Let us say, for example, that you have to call on twenty prospects to get five presentations. This would give you a ratio of 20 to 5 for your prospecting activities. Selling is very much a numbers game.

Now, let us say that you have to make five presentations to get two prospects who are interested enough in your offering that you can follow up on them. This would give you a ratio of 5 to 2 for your presentation activities.

In the third part of the sales funnel you have following up and closing. Let us say that you have to follow up with two prospects to get one sale.

What this means is that you have to put twenty prospects in the top of the funnel to get one sale out of the bottom of the funnel, a ratio of 20 to 1. The rule, therefore, is this: "Keep your funnel full."

Apply the 80/20 Rule to your sales activities. Spend 80 percent of your time prospecting and presenting, and spend only 20 percent of your time following up. And don't mix them up. Avoid the temptation to spend all your time calling back on prospects who won't give you a yes or a no. Instead, spend most of your time filling your sales funnel with new prospects.

Here is a great rule for sales success: *Spend more time with better prospects!*

Prospecting Power

The definition of a good prospect is "Someone who can and will buy and pay within a reasonable period of time."

Do not waste your precious selling time with nice people who do not have the authority, money, or ability to buy from you. Think continually about your personal income, and always be sure that the person you are talking to can contribute to that income soon enough to justify the time you are investing in him or her.

Prospecting begins with your analyzing your product or service and your market so that you can be clear about what you are really selling and the type of person who is most likely to buy it.

Begin with the question, What do I sell? Answer this question in terms of what it *does* for your customer, not what it *is*. Define the exact benefits or advantages that your customer will enjoy by purchasing what you sell. How will he or she be better off?

What specific ways does your product or service improve the customer's life or work?

Second, why should the customer buy the product or service from you or your company? What is your competitive advantage? What is it about what you sell that makes it better, superior in some way, to that of your competition? How are you different? What is your unique selling proposition?

Surprisingly enough, most salespeople don't know the answers to these questions. As a result, their sales efforts are scattered rather than focused, and their sales results are far below what they should be. The sad fact is that even a qualified prospect cannot buy from you until and unless he or she knows why what you sell is better than someone else's product or service. Clarity is essential.

Segment Your Market

Once you are absolutely clear about what you sell, defined from the customer's point of view, and you know why and how what you sell is better than anything else available for a particular type of customer, your next job is to identify exactly those customers who can most benefit, the most rapidly, from what you sell.

Here are some of the qualities of a good prospect. Your job at the first contact or meeting is to determine if the person you are talking to fits this description:

1. The prospect has a genuine need that your product/service can fill.
2. The prospect is friendly toward you and has a favorable impression of your company and industry.
3. The prospect values the results/benefits of what you sell more than the amount you charge.
4. The prospect is willing and able to make a buying decision in the near future.
5. The prospect is a good potential source of further sales and referrals.

Your job is to ask questions early in the sales process to determine how many of these qualities the prospect possesses.

Wasting Your Time

Some people are a complete waste of time. Even if you can get appointments with them, they will seldom, if ever, buy anything from you. Here are some qualities of poor prospects:

1. The prospect has no need, no money, no authority, or no urgency to buy or use what you sell.
2. The prospect is critical of you, your company, or your product.

3. The prospect immediately haggles and complains about your price.
4. The prospect compares you unfavorably to your competitors.
5. The prospect is indecisive about purchasing from you or anyone.
6. The prospect is not a good source of resales or referrals.

Sometimes the best use of your time is to break off discussions with a poor prospect before you waste too much time going down a blind alley. Always be polite, but don't spend time where your efforts are not appreciated.

Getting More Appointments with Better Prospects

In your market, there exist what are called "high-probability prospects." These are people who have an immediate need for what you are selling. Your job is to find as many of them as possible, as soon as possible, and leave the "low-probability prospects" for others.

The very best way to prospect is, first, be clear about the most important and valuable benefit your product can give your customer. Second, be clear about how and why your product is ideal and appropriate for a specific type of customer. Third, focus and concentrate all your efforts on finding and talking to more of this type of customer.

Remember, the customer's first question is, Why should I listen to you? Your job is to answer this question in your first communication, whether it is by telephone, voice mail, fax, letter, or e-mail. Summarize the primary benefit of your offering, for a qualified, high-probability prospect, in your first words.

For example, when I was selling sales training, I would call a company and ask to speak to the person who was responsible for sales, whose income was probably determined by how much was sold (the "problem haver"). When that person came on the line, I would say, "Hello. My name is Brian Tracy from the Institute for Executive Development. I was calling to find out if you would be interested in a method to increase your sales by 20 to 30 percent over the next three to six months."

This opening fulfills all the requirements of a professional call. You identify yourself immediately and give your name and your company's. You then politely ask the "qualifying question." If this person is a prospect for what you are selling, he or she will reply by saying something like "Of course. What is it?"

When you are speaking to the right person and you have asked a question that connects with an existing need, the prospect will ask, "What is it?" If he or she says anything else, the chances are good that this person is not a prospect for what you are selling, or your opening words need to be changed.

Another example is in the sale of financial services. One of the most powerful qualifying questions is always, "Would you like to see a way to reduce your taxes on your existing income?"

Everyone with any income is interested in reducing his or her taxes. A qualified prospect will always ask, "What is it?"

You can develop an opening question or statement that triggers immediate interest from a person who can and will buy what you are selling. This requires some imagination and experimentation, but the results can be amazing.

Your job is to spend more time with better prospects. You must therefore be absolutely clear about what it is you sell and exactly who your best prospects are the most likely to be. In today's market, you must learn to focus your sales efforts, to become a rifle rather than a machine gun. This is the way you keep your sales funnel full.

You should have far more prospects in your funnel than you have time to see, even if you work all day long. Never allow yourself to run out of prospects. Keep your funnel full. Remember the ratios. You have to call on a lot of prospects to get a small number of sales.

Be sure the ones you are calling on are the ones you can sell to the most easily.

ACTION EXERCISES

Develop a powerful opening statement or question that will immediately grab the attention and interest of a good prospect for what you sell. Try it out and test it until it works every single time.

Begin today to keep an accurate record of the number of people you call each day, the number of sales appointments you get from these calls, the number of sales you get from these appointments, and the dollar value of each sale. Use a simple recording method such as four vertical lines with a diagonal line crossed through them for every five people in each category.

Make a plan today to improve your ratios between prospecting calls and presentations and between presentations and eventual sales. If your current ratio is 20 to 1, see if you can't get a little better in each area. Work to increase your sales rate to 15 to 1, then 10 to 1, and so on. Never stop improving in the critical things you do that determine your level of sales. And keep your sales funnel full.

Set Clear Income and Sales Goals

There is one quality that one must possess to win, and that is definiteness of purpose, the knowledge of what one wants and a burning desire to possess it.

—NAPOLEON HILL

Your ability to set goals and then to make clear, written plans for their accomplishment is the master skill of success. In no area is this more important than in the field of professional sales.

The fact is that you can't hit a target that you can't see. The highest paid salespeople, in every field, have very clear sales and income goals, broken down by year, month, week, day, and even by the hour. They know exactly what they have to do every working day to achieve the goals they have set for themselves. Every morning, they get up and get to work on reaching their sales goals.

Here is a powerful process you can use to move yourself into the top 20 percent in your industry: Begin by deciding how much you want to earn in the next twelve months. Set a goal to increase your income by at least 25 percent over your best year. This kind of a "stretch" goal will motivate and energize you to perform at a higher level than ever before. And the only question you need to ask is, How?

Let us say that your income goal for next year is to earn $50,000. For the sake of this example, let us assume that you earn an average of 5 percent commission on sales. This means that you will have to sell $1,000,000 worth of your product or service next year in order to earn $50,000.

You can now break these numbers down by the number of months, weeks, and days that you intend to work. This will tell you that you will have to sell $83,333 per month of your product to sell $1,000,000 worth in twelve months. By selling this amount, you will earn approximately $4,200 per month, or $50,000 over the year.

You can now break your income and sales goals down by the week and even by the amount you need to sell each day. This will give you specific targets to aim at for the next twelve months.

Here is an even simpler method you can use. Take your $50,000 income goal and divide it by the number 250, the days you work in an average year. This comes out to $200 per day. Then divide the $200 per day by

8, the number of hours you work in an average day. This will give you the amount of $25 per hour.

(Another way you can calculate your desired hourly rate is to divide your income goal by 2,000, the number of hours the average salesperson works in a year. Your answer will be the same.)

Now you know that to earn $50,000 per year, you must earn $25 per hour, every hour, 8 hours per day, 250 days a year.

From this moment forward, you must discipline yourself to *work all the time you work.* Absolutely refuse to do anything during your workday that does not pay $25 per hour. You must refuse to make your own photocopies, read the newspaper, or chat with your coworkers. You do not drop off your dry cleaning, pick up your laundry, get your car washed, phone your friends, or go shopping. None of these activities pay $25 per hour. No one will pay you $25 per hour to do them.

In selling, only three things you can do during the day pay $25 per hour or more. These three activities are *prospect, present,* and *follow up!*

The average salesperson, according to Columbia University, works only about one and one-half hours per day. The first sales call, on average, is usually made at about 11:00 A.M. The last sales call is usually made at about 3:30 P.M. In between, the average salesperson talks with coworkers, drinks coffee, reads the paper, phones his or her friends, goes for lunch, and drives around listening to music. As a result, the average salesperson works only about 20 percent of the time.

If you want to be in the top 20 percent of your field, you can only get there by making more sales. You can lead the field only by spending more time in the specific sales activities of prospecting, presenting, and following up that lead to sales success.

Ask yourself, every minute, "Is what I'm doing right now leading to a sale?" If what you are doing is not leading to a sale, you must immediately stop doing it and get back to work.

And when is a salesperson working? There are only three times. You are working only when you are *prospecting, presenting,* and *following up.*

You can use this proven formula to double your income: Simply double the amount of "face time" that you spend with prospects and customers. Plan every day carefully to maximize the number of minutes you spend across from people who can buy what you are selling. If the average salesperson is spending 90 minutes with prospects each day, by increasing your average to 180 minutes, you will make twice as much as the people around you.

A popular management principle says, "What gets measured gets done." The very act of measuring the number of minutes you spend each day face-to-face with people who can buy will immediately increase your awareness, improve your time management skills, and boost your income.

◆

ACTION EXERCISES

Take a sheet of paper and write a list of ten goals that you would like to achieve over the next year. Review this list and select the one goal that would have the most positive impact on your life if you were to achieve it. Write this goal at the top of a new sheet of paper. This becomes your major definite purpose.

Now, set a deadline on your major goal, and set subdeadlines as well. Make a list of everything you can think of that you can do to achieve this goal. Organize this list into a plan with priorities. Finally, take action on this plan immediately, and do something every single day that moves you toward this goal.

Your commitment to yourself and your future, represented by written goals and plans, will increase your results faster than you can imagine.

Manage Your Territory Well

Our goals can only be reached through
a vehicle of a plan, in which we must
fervently believe, and upon which
we must fervently act.
There is no other route to success.

—STEPHEN A. BRENNEN

Just as a retail shopkeeper has a store from which he or she sells, you have a store as well. It is your sales territory. It is the area in which you work to develop sales and customers. And just as a physical store must be well organized for maximum sales results, so must your territory.

One of the major reasons for failure in selling is poor territory management. The average salesperson travels randomly throughout his or her territory, driving from place to place depending on whoever calls or is willing to see him or her at the moment.

This salesperson will often drive all the way up to the north end of the city to make one call and then all the way down to the south end of the city, spending an hour or more in traffic, to make the second call. Then he or she drives all the way back to the north end again for the next call.

You know that your income is largely determined by the amount of time that you spend personally with people who can buy. You must therefore plan every day strategically to increase these precious moments, and let nothing distract or divert you.

Here is a simple method of territory management that you can apply immediately. Divide your sales territory into four parts, like cutting up a pie. From now on, resolve to work in one of these quadrants each day or each half day. When you make appointments, cluster your appointments so that they are close together. This will shorten the amount of time you spend on the road and increase the number of minutes of each day when you are actually prospecting, presenting, and following up.

If someone asks you if you can meet on a particular day and you are not scheduled to be in that area on that day, resist the temptation to change your plans and rush over. Instead, explain politely that you will be in the prospect's area on a particular morning or afternoon, and ask to arrange an appointment at that time. It is amazing how much more respect prospects have for a salesperson when they know that he or she is busy and well organized.

Many salespeople, by reorganizing their territories, have increased their income by 20 percent, 30 percent, and even 50 percent in a single month. They find themselves spending much less time traveling and much more time face-to-face with customers. Both their income and their self-confidence go up.

Remember, your time is all you have to sell. And nobody will pay you for the time you spend driving around between appointments. It is not the number of hours that you put in each day that counts but the amount of direct selling work you put into those hours.

To increase your income, you must increase the number of minutes that you spend face-to-face with customers by reducing your traveling time. Put the law of averages to work in your behalf. The more people you see, all other things being equal, the more you will sell.

ACTION EXERCISES

Take full responsibility for planning and organizing the territory in which you work. Get a map of the area and study it carefully. Divide the map into four quadrants based on your experience with the area and the natural dividing lines, such as streets.

When you prospect, set a goal to schedule a full day or half day of appointments in a specific sector. Phone people only in that quadrant until your appointment book is full. Then go on to fill your calendar with appointments in each of the other quadrants.

Practice the Seven Secrets of Sales Success

Do a little bit more than average and
from that point on your progress
multiplies itself out of all proportion
to the effort put in.

—PAUL J. MEYER

Sales success is based on seven secrets, or principles. They are practiced by all the highest paid salespeople every day. The regular application of these principles is virtually guaranteed to move you to the top of your field.

Success secret number one: **Get serious!** Make a decision to go all the way to the top of your field. Make a decision today to join the top 10 percent. No one and nothing can hold you back from being the best except yourself. Remember, it takes just as long to be great as to be mediocre. The time is going to pass anyway. Your job is to commit to excellence, to get better and better each day, and to never, never stop until you reach the summit.

Success secret number two: **Identify the skill that's limiting your sales success.** Identify your weakest important skill and then make a plan to become absolutely excellent in that area. Ask yourself, and your boss, *"What one skill, if I developed and did it consistently in an excellent fashion, would have the greatest positive impact on my sales?"* Whatever your answer to this question, write it down, set a deadline, make a plan, and then work on it every day. This decision alone can change your life.

Success secret number three: **Get around the right people.** Get around positive, successful people. Associate with men and women who are going somewhere with their lives. And get away from negative, critical, complaining people. They drag you down, tire you out, distract and discourage you, and lead you inevitably to underachievement and failure. Remember, you cannot fly with the eagles if you continue to scratch with the turkeys.

Success secret number four: **Take excellent care of your physical health.** You need high levels of energy to sell effectively and to bounce back from continual rejection and discouragement. Be sure to eat the right foods, get the right amount of exercise, and get plenty of rest and recreation. Make a decision that you are going to live to be eighty years old or more, and begin today to do whatever you have to do to achieve that goal.

Success secret number five: **Visualize yourself as one of the top people in your field.** Imagine yourself performing at your best all day long. Feed your subconscious mind with vivid, exciting, emotionalized pictures of yourself as positive, confident, competent, and completely in control of every part of your life. These clear mental pictures preprogram you and motivate you to sell at your best in any situation.

Success secret number six: **Practice positive self-talk continually.** Control your inner dialogue. Talk to yourself the way you want to be rather than the way you are today.

For example, repeat to yourself these powerful words, over and over again: "I like myself! I'm the best! I can do it! I love my work!"

Say to yourself, "I feel happy! I feel healthy! I feel terrific!"

Remember, fully 95 percent of your emotions are determined by the way you talk to yourself, most of the time. The way you feel determines how you behave. And how you behave determines how much you sell.

Your job is to get yourself on an upward spiral where you think and talk to yourself positively, all day long. Think, walk, talk, and act like the very best people in your field. When you do, your success becomes inevitable.

Success secret number seven: **Take positive action toward your goals, every single day.** Be proactive rather than reactive. Grab the bull by the horns. If you are not happy with your income, get out and get face-to-face with more customers. If you are not happy with any part of your life, accept responsibility and take charge.

All successful salespeople are intensely action oriented. They have a sense of urgency. They develop a bias for action. They "do it now!" They have a compulsion to reach closure. They maintain a fast tempo and move quickly in everything they do.

And the good news is this: The faster you move, the more energy you have. The faster you move, the more ground you cover. The faster you move, the more people you see. The more people you see, the more experience you get. The more experience you get, the more sales you make. The more people you see and the more sales you make, the more your self-esteem and self-respect go up and the more you will feel great about yourself. You will have more energy. You will be happier and more positive.

The faster you move, the more you take complete control of your entire life. You virtually guarantee that you will be one of the top performers and the highest paid people in your field.

Conclusion:
Pulling It All Together

I started my life with very few benefits or advantages. I worked at laboring jobs and worried about money all the time. I bless the day that I got into selling. The field of selling offered me, and offers you, all the great joys, benefits, and possibilities that life has to offer. And the better you become at selling, the more respected and important you become to your company, to your community, and to your world.

Salespeople are among the most important people in America. Every single company depends for its survival on the success of its salespeople. High sales is the number one reason for company success. Low sales is the number one reason for company failure. And you can be in the driver's seat.

Over the past thirty years, I have trained more than 500,000 salespeople in twenty-three countries. I have trained people who have come to the United

States with no money, no friends, no contacts, and, very often, no ability to speak English. But they have taken these ideas, practiced them over and over again, and gone onto become sales leaders in major national organizations.

The Law of Cause and Effect is the iron law of human destiny. In effect, it says that anything that anyone else has done, you can do as well. All you have to do is find out what he or she did and then do the same over and over yourself until you master it.

Remember, no one is better than you and no one is smarter than you. People who are doing better than you simply have learned and applied the principles of success earlier than you. They have learned the twenty-one great ways to be a sales superstar and they practice them every single day. When you begin practicing these ideas yourself, you will see the results almost immediately. Once more, here they are:

1. **Commit to Excellence:** Make a decision today to become one of the very best salespeople in your field. Get going and keep going until you achieve your goal.

2. **Act As If It Were Impossible to Fail:** Do the thing you fear and the death of fear is certain. Resolve today to face whatever fears of failure and rejection might be holding you back, and do what you fear anyway!

3. **Put Your Whole Heart into Your Selling:**
   Make a 100 percent total commitment to your
   profession of selling, to your company, to
   your products and services, and to your customers. Put your whole heart into your work.

4. **Position Yourself as a Real Professional:**
   See yourself as a consultant, an advisor, and
   a valuable resource to your customers.
   Conduct yourself as a consultant would, in
   every customer interaction.

5. **Prepare Thoroughly for Every Call:** Do your
   homework before you see a customer for the
   first time. Find out everything you can about
   the customer and his or her business so you
   can be of the greatest service to the customer.

6. **Dedicate Yourself to Continuous Learning:**
   Learn something new each day that can help
   you to be more skilled and effective in selling.
   Read, listen to audio programs, and take additional training.

7. **Accept Complete Responsibility for Results:**
   See yourself as the president of your own personal sales corporation, completely in charge
   of your own life and sales activities. Instead of
   making excuses, focus on making progress in
   your sales work.

8. **Become Brilliant on the Basics:** Learn and
   practice the fundamentals of the sales process.

Use them in the proper order, every single
time. Never allow yourself to get distracted
or to take shortcuts.

9. **Build Long-Term Relationships:** The more
    the customer likes you as a person, the easier
    it is for you to sell. Ask good questions, listen
    attentively to the answers, and focus on the
    person before the sale.

10. **Be a Financial Improvement Specialist:**
    Look for ways to demonstrate to your prospect
    that your product or service has a definite
    return on investment, that he or she will be
    better off financially by buying and using it.

11. **Use Educational Selling with Every
    Customer:** Take the time to learn how your
    product or service can most help your cus-
    tomer. Then teach your customer how he or
    she can get the most benefit and enjoyment
    out of what you sell.

12. **Build Megacredibility with Every Prospect:**
    Everything counts! Be sure that you look the
    part of a believable and trustworthy sales
    professional. Use testimonials from satisfied
    customers. Build credibility with everything
    you do and say.

13. **Handle Objections Effectively:** Learn how
    to resolve customer concerns and overcome
    hesitation in the sales conversation. Be

prepared with well-thought-out answers to every question.

14. **Deal with Price Professionally:** Be proud of your product and your prices. Concentrate on showing your prospect that what you sell is valuable and worth every cent that you are asking.

15. **Know How to Close the Sale:** Learn and practice proven sales closing techniques. The future belongs to the askers—those people who boldly ask for what they want—especially to those who ask the customer to take action on the offer.

16. **Make Every Minute Count:** Your time is your most precious resource; it's all you really have to sell. Work all the time you work. Don't waste time on idle chatter or low-value activities.

17. **Apply the 80/20 Rule to Everything:** Spend more and more of your time on your most valuable prospects and customers. Allocate your time based on the potential value of the activity, the top 20 percent of the things you do.

18. **Keep Your Sales Funnel Full:** Your job consists of three main activities. They are *prospecting, presenting,* and *following up.* Your income is determined by how often and

how well you perform these three tasks.
Concentrate on them all day long.

19. **Set Clear Income and Sales Goals:** Decide
exactly how much you want to earn per hour
and how much you will have to sell to earn
that amount. Never do anything during the
working day that does not pay you your
desired hourly rate.

20. **Manage Your Territory Well:** Cluster your
calls so that you can spend less time traveling
and more time face-to-face with people who
can and will buy your products or services.

21. **Practice the Seven Secrets of Sales Success:**
Keep yourself positive and motivated all day
long by thinking continually about how you
can get better and better in the key areas that
determine your success and your income.

Remember, there are no limits to what you can accomplish with your time and your life, except for the
limits you place on yourself.

Good luck!

Learning Resources of Brian Tracy International

BRIAN TRACY'S
PERSONAL COACHING PROGRAMS
The Keys to Making a Quantum Leap
in Your Life and Career

❖ **Focal Point Advanced Coaching
and Mentoring Program**

Brian Tracy offers a personal coaching program in San Diego for successful entrepreneurs, self-employed professionals, and top salespeople. Participants learn how to apply the Focal Point Process to every part of their work and personal lives.

Participants learn a step-by-step process of personal strategic planning that enables them to take complete control of their time and their lives. Over the course of the program, participants meet with Brian Tracy one full day every three months. During these sessions, they learn how to double their income and double their time off.

They identify what they enjoy doing the most and learn how to become better in their most profitable activities. Participants learn how to delegate, downsize, eliminate, and get rid of all the tasks they neither enjoy nor benefit from. They learn how to identify their special talents and how to use leverage and concentration to move to the top of their fields.

❖ Focal Point Personal Telephone Coaching Program

Brian Tracy's personally trained professional coaches work with you step by step to help you move to the next level of performance in your career.

This intensive twelve-week program comes complete with exercises, audio programs, prework, and personalized coaching.

You learn how to implement the Focal Point Process in every area of your life. Working with a trusted mentor, you develop complete clarity about who you are, what you want, where you are going, and the fastest ways to achieve all your goals.

> For more information on the in-person or telephone coaching and mentoring programs offered by Brian Tracy, visit www.briantracy.com, call 858-481-2977, or write to Brian Tracy International, 462 Stevens Avenue, Suite 202, Solana Beach, CA 92075.

Visit Brian Tracy at www.21successsecrets.com for a *free copy* of his new audio program, "The 21 Success Secrets of Self-Made Millionaires." You pay only shipping and handling! Also, check out Brian Tracy's recent books, *Eat That Frog!* and *The 100 Absolutely Unbreakable Laws of Business Success,* at your local bookstore or at **www.briantracy.com**.

BRIAN TRACY AUDIO LEARNING PROGRAMS

	AUDIO	CD
❖ **Psychology of Selling** (7 hours) The most powerful, practical, professional selling program in the world today.	$75.00	$80.00
❖ **Advanced Selling Techniques** (7 hours) The most complete advanced selling program for top professionals in the world.	$75.00	$80.00
❖ **How to Master Your Time** (7 hours) More than 500 key ideas for time management in a proven system that brings about immediate results. Save 2 hours every day.	$65.00	$70.00
❖ **Million-Dollar Habits** (7 hours) The specific habits and behaviors practiced by high earners and self-made millionaires. Double and triple your income.	$65.00	$70.00
❖ **Master Strategies for High Achievement** (7 hours) More than 150 of the key strategies practiced by the most successful people—in every area of life.	$65.00	$70.00
❖ **24 Techniques for Closing the Sale** (65 minutes) Now you can double, triple, or even reach 100 percent on your closing rate using 24 of the finest closing techniques ever devised. These techniques are so effective and so well explained that you'll be using them after the first viewing of this classic tour de force of sales techniques.	VIDEO	$80.00

❖ SPECIAL OFFER ❖

- Any 1 program—$65
- 2–3 programs—$60 each
- 4–5 programs—$55 each
- All 6 programs—$295

To order one or more of these programs, phone 800/542-4252, visit our Web site at **www.briantracy.com**, or write to Brian Tracy International, 462 Stevens Avenue, Suite 202, Solana Beach, CA 92075. Fax: 858/481-2445. **Unconditionally guaranteed for one full year or your money back!** If you are not delighted with these learning programs, return the materials for a complete refund any time in the year following the date of purchase.

BRIAN TRACY
SPEAKER · AUTHOR · TRAINER

Brian Tracy is one of the most popular professional speakers in the world. He addresses more than 250,000 people each year in talks and seminars, from keynote addresses to sessions three to four days in length.

His topics include

- High Performance Leadership
  for the 21st Century
- Maximizing Personal Performance
- Advanced Selling Skills and Strategies
- Counter Attack! for Salespeople and Businesses

For more information, visit www.briantracy.com. Register for a free subscription to one or more of Brian's helpful newsletters on Personal Success, Time Management, and Financial Mastery.

To book Brian as a speaker, contact
Brian Tracy International
462 Stevens Avenue, Suite 202
Solana Beach, CA 92075
Phone 858-481-2977, x17
Fax 858-481-2445
www.briantracy.com

Visit **www.briantracy.com** and
sign up for a **Free Subscription** to
Brian's weekly Sales Success Newsletter!

Index

About the Author

Brian Tracy is the top sales speaker, trainer, and consultant in the world today. He addresses more than 250,000 men and women each year in public and private seminars attended by as many as 20,000 people at one time. He has spoken to overflow audiences in every large and small city in the United States and Canada, as well as twenty-two other countries.

Brian has worked with over 500 companies since he began teaching and training in 1981. Prior to founding Brian Tracy International, he worked in twenty-two different businesses, selling everything from soap and Christmas trees to investments and commercial real estate. He has started and built numerous sales forces in a variety of industries. He has developed a series of high-impact audio and video sales training programs that have been translated into sixteen languages and are used in twenty-three countries.

Brian teaches a no-nonsense, straightforward approach to selling based on building high-quality relationships, coupled with a strong focus on helping customers get what they really want in a fast, cost-effective way. He has written twenty-four books and given more than 1,000 radio and television interviews on the subjects of personal and professional success.

Brian Tracy is the president of Brian Tracy International, headquartered in Solana Beach, California. He is married with four children and is active in social and community affairs.